The Real JRR Tolkien

This book is dedicated to the wonderful friends and family members who have supported and believed in me over the years, including but not limited to the people named below. Without you I would not be able to write. Thank you!

To Vic, a dear friend and the best Dwarven scholar this Orkish scholar could know!

To Jaime, for being the first pairs of eyes on this monstrosity, and to Avery, EK, and Helen, without whose '@s', belief, perspectives and encouragement I would not even have pitched for this, and to all of my 9W friends for the confidence, inspiration and support you give me every day.

To Penny and Cliodhna, for your belief in me, for being wonderful friends and being the best dungeoneers this DM could ever have (alongside Vic!).

To Sebastian, for your friendship, compassion and wisdom.

And to Ms McPhoenix, Ms Jack Thompson and Mr Hinchliffe, the English teachers who inspired me throughout my schooling.

The Real JRR Tolkien

The Man Who Created Middle-Earth

Jesse Xander

WHITE
OWL

First published in Great Britain in 2021 by
White Owl
An imprint of
Pen & Sword Books Ltd
Yorkshire – Philadelphia

ISBN 978 1 52676 515 4

A CIP catalogue record for this book is
available from the British Library.

Typeset by Mac Style
Printed and bound by CPI Group (UK) Ltd, Croydon, CR0 4YY

Pen & Sword Books Limited incorporates the imprints of Atlas,
Archaeology, Aviation, Discovery, Family History, Fiction, History,
Maritime, Military, Military Classics, Politics, Select, Transport,
True Crime, Air World, Frontline Publishing, Leo Cooper, Remember
When, Seaforth Publishing, The Praetorian Press, Wharncliffe
Local History, Wharncliffe Transport, Wharncliffe True Crime
and White Owl.

For a complete list of Pen & Sword titles please contact

PEN & SWORD BOOKS LIMITED
47 Church Street, Barnsley, South Yorkshire, S70 2AS, England
E-mail: enquiries@pen-and-sword.co.uk
Website: www.pen-and-sword.co.uk

Or

PEN AND SWORD BOOKS
1950 Lawrence Rd, Havertown, PA 19083, USA
E-mail: Uspen-and-sword@casematepublishers.com
Website: www.penandswordbooks.com

Contents

Acknowledgements

The author would like to thank and give credit to the following people, institutes, organisations and companies, who generously provided their resources and/or expertise towards the creation of this book:

Book production process: Kate Bohdanowicz, Jaime Starr, Vic Roth, Lori Jones, Aileen Pringle, Jon Wilkinson, Gaynor Haliday and the rest of the Pen & Sword Books team.

Research resources: The King Edward's Foundation archive, The British Library, The Tolkien Estate, St Anne's College Oxford.

Quotations: Humphrey Carpenter, Colin Duriez, John Garth, an anonymous historian on behalf of the GCHQ, H. Harrod, *Crist of Cynewulf* (Lines 104 to 108), The King Edward's Foundation archive, Peter Hastings, Joseph Wright FBE, C. Sladen, Anna Smoll, Christopher Wiseman, Sir Stanley Unwin, CS Lewis, Edith Tolkien, Hilary Tolkien, Mabel Tolkien, J.R.R. Tolkien and The Tolkien Estate.

Images: Tanya Dedyukhina, Gentry Graves, The King Edward's Foundation archive, Stefan Servos, Jonathan P. Bowen, The British Library, Earthsound, Olaf Studt, Michal 'miszka' Nowakowski, Elliott and Fry, Nabitbitcom, Antikwar, Strebe, Anna Tochennikova, MNStudio, Eeli Purola, James Jensen, PictureLake, Sancho Proudfoot, Anupam Hatui. Credit is also given to The Tolkien Gateway, Wikimedia Commons, ShutterStock, VectorStock, iStock, and the public domain.

The author has to the best of their knowledge and ability respected the licensing and copyright of the copyright holders, and has adhered to their licences in the reproduction of these images for this book.

Introduction: On Leaf-Moulds

Who doesn't love a good story? The answer, scientifically speaking, is almost no-one. Whether we read fiction, non-fiction, magazines, or simply love watching television or listening to well-told anecdotes, it is human nature to narrativise the world as we see it. Everything, from sweeping fantasy fiction to the factual news stories, will follow a narrative structure. It's how we prefer to ingest information.

But why is this relevant? For two reasons: the first, that this innate human desire to tell a story rather than lay out bare facts makes the art of biography a tough needle to thread, and the second, is that that tightrope of factual complexity and flowing narrative was where Tolkien lived, and where he created his best works. What makes *The Lord of the Rings, The Hobbit* and *Silmarillion* so engaging, even after all these years, is that they are works of complete fiction with the multifarious nature of factual events. There are competing viewpoints, overlapping mythologies, diverse cultures, calendars, and languages... Middle-Earth truly lives up to its name; it is a world, and it feels alive.

And part of the reason why this is, is that Tolkien himself lived it. For decades he worked to uncover a history of a place that didn't exist, and I am not being hyperbolic when I say that he himself referred to the 'discovery' of Middle-Earth.[1] The world in the books feels organic because to Tolkien it was.

But what motivates a man to dedicate his life to what even some of his closest friends saw as a foolish dream?[2] That is something that this book hopes to answer in part, but also to avoid in some ways. For all too often biographers, documentarians, interviewers, etc., fall into the trap of viewing authors – especially those known for a singular work or series – as incubators of their works, rather than as whole people: looking past the humanity of the author and replacing it with portents to their works. This book is written in quite the opposite manner; the 'story' is one of John Ronald Reuel Tolkien, the man, and his life. His works feature in it, of course, but they were only one facet of a complex individual.

Writing a biography in this way, combing through records for the personality and beliefs of someone, can of course lead to uncomfortable discoveries. To see someone's humanity is to see both their strengths and their flaws, and this book glosses over neither. This 'story's' protagonist is a complex person, whose creativity and kindness is recorded alongside his documented prejudices, and practices that may be considered vices. But to not do so would be to do Tolkien, and ourselves, a grave disservice; we learn nothing from manufacturing the illusion that people who create things we love cannot be wrong, or hold troubling beliefs, and even less from insisting that said beliefs don't in some way influence the works we adore. To analyse people and their work, to engage in literary criticism and respectfully critical biography, is to go from passive consumers to active listeners and creators. When we can cast a discerning eye on media, including the media we love, we can truly learn from it: both what makes it so resonant or inspiring, and what holds it back, or even makes some elements of it potentially harmful. What makes Middle-Earth so enduring and fascinating is its complexity, so it seems only right to approach the topic of its author with the same depth and nuance.

The secondary goal of this biography is to look at the inspirations for Middle-Earth. Not to view Tolkien's life as a hollow shell through which the world hatched, but instead to look for small details, little motifs, interests and recurring passions, which were the seedlings that became Middle-Earth. As Tolkien himself described his process:

> 'One writes such a story not out of the leaves of trees still to be observed, nor by means of botany and soil-science; but it grows like a seed in the dark out of the leaf-mould of the mind: out of all that has been seen or thought or read, that has long ago been forgotten, descending into the deeps. No doubt there is much selection, as with a gardener: what one throws on one's personal compost-heap.'[3]

This was perhaps why he was so resistant to analysis of himself and biography in his lifetime: to him it looked like sifting through soil whilst ignoring a beautiful orchard. But here we differ, perhaps because of our academic backgrounds. Tolkien was a linguist, and I am a biological anthropologist. The study of people and mould (both metaphorical and literal) is profoundly interesting to me, just as much as the orchards that grow from them. To continue his metaphor: if an author writing a story is a gardener growing a seedling from their leaf-mould, then soil-science would be the analysis of the author's life in relation to their work. As such, consider this book a kind of literary soil-science: an account of things found in a rich and varied mulch, with special attention paid to anything still wriggling around on the slide!

Someone who merely analyses soil is not so much a lead scientist as a laboratory assistant, and that certainly fits with how writing this work feels. To write a biography on such a celebrated figure, with scores of academic papers and books written about him, and even a whole field of study dedicated to analysing his life, makes anything I have written feel incredibly small, the assistant's notes to be incorporated into a larger paper. I am standing on the shoulders of giants, and am indebted to the scholars that came before me, in particular Humphrey Carpenter, Tolkien's only official biographer, who had access to his diaries, and to my mind penned one of the best biographies on any literary figure to date. Additional thanks go to Colin Duriez for his modern biography and acute eye for finding details that make Tolkien come to life, John Garth for his rigorous academic look at Tolkien's young adulthood, and Christina Scull and Wayne G. Hammond for their astonishingly detailed chronology. And, of course, I am grateful to Tolkien himself, for recording so many of his thoughts and letters, and to his son Christopher, for curating such a wide variety of his papers, and graciously allowing them to be released to the public.

But the final ingredient of any text – even non-fiction – is the author themself. After reading many a Tolkien biography, I noticed that most have a story about how the biographer found Tolkien's work, and most were fans since childhood, and very adoring of hobbits and elves. Whilst I do have a story about how I found Tolkien, it differs considerably from those of my colleagues. My father read me *The Hobbit* when I was a young child, and I enjoyed it well enough, but it did not capture my imagination in the way the *Narnia Chronicles*, read to me by my mother, had some months before. My only memory of my encounter with *The Hobbit* at that time was that I enjoyed the trolls and Gollum. Fast-forward several years to when I was 12 and my father and I watched *The Lord of the Rings* trilogy box set on DVD. Again, I enjoyed it, and I had been gorging on other fantasy books and films in the interim years, and I remember asking about the part of the world that piqued my interest to beyond mere enjoyment, 'What are the Orcs?' Upon receiving a 'just Sauron's henchmen' from my father, the next time I would show any further interest in Middle-Earth was when a friend lent me *The Fellowship of the Ring* when I was 16. I read it and enjoyed it well enough, but when the same friend offered me *The Two Towers* I politely declined.

It wasn't until I was 20 that I found my foothold in Middle-Earth, and by then two things had changed. The first, my guide was no longer my father who mainly liked hobbits, but my close friend who was interested in the whole of Middle-Earth, and Dwarves in particular. Secondly, I was now studying anthropology, and was particularly drawn to how responsible anthropology can be used to challenge the bias of historical sources (e.g. deconstructing colonial sources to uncover at least some of the erased histories of oppressed or even eradicated communities). So it was with this mindset that my friend took me to see *The Hobbit: An Unexpected Journey*. And I finally understood why so many people fall in love with Middle-Earth. The world was so much more than the sum of its parts. Hobbits, Elves, Dwarves, Orcs and humans weren't merely flat pawns set out to tell a single story: they were whole communities with histories and cultures and conflicting historical sources, varying religions, individual goals… it was a fantasy world that withstood real-world analysis. We saw *An Unexpected Journey* five more times in the cinema. I devoured the books, and studying commenced. My friend and I studied Middle-Earth's historical sources, their bias, their languages… Orkish and Khuzdhul and Sindarin and Quenya rattle around my mind as Russian, French, Latin, Middle Egyptian and the other real languages I've studied have. It has been seven years since I first journeyed into Middle-Earth, and I have no intention of slowing down. There are too many stories to uncover, too much history gone unanalysed, too much fun to be had.

I hope that this unconventional passion for Middle-Earth, for analysis, and for leaf-moulds, is captured in this biography.

Mx Jesse Xander

Chapter 1

A Sickly Boy in Bloemfontein

J.R.R. Tolkien's story starts with music and a remarkable woman. The woman is Mabel Suffield, who, in spring of 1891 left England on the steamer ship *Roslin Castle* to sail to South Africa. She was 21, and travelling to the other side of the equator to culminate what was (for the time) the end of a long engagement of three years to a man thirteen years her senior: Arthur Tolkien.

From the Tolkiens came the music, generations past, at least. The Tolkiens were upright-piano makers, and although Arthur's sisters could play the upright that carried the family name at parties, where Mabel and Arthur bonded during their long engagement, the Tolkiens were no longer the current owners of the firm. Arthur's father had left his children no business to inherit, so Arthur had worked at the Lloyds Bank. However, his prospects in the Birmingham office were slow-going, and if he were to prove to the disapproving Suffields that he could indeed provide for Mabel, he would have to travel.

The inscription on the lid of the piano his sisters played at parties that read, 'Irresistible Piano-Forte: Manufactured Expressly for Extreme Climates',[1] which might have seemed silly in their home in Birmingham, now became prescient; for not a year after proposing to Mabel, Arthur had obtained a position in the Bank of Africa.

In some ways it was fortunate that Mabel's father had forbidden their union at the culmination of their betrothal, for indeed at the start of his South African banking career Arthur was in no position to provide a stable home for his beloved, for he travelled any which way between the Cape and Johannesburg, filling in temporary roles for the bank. However, in 1890, he managed to land the branch manager position for the Bloemfontein bank. By January of 1891, Mabel was 21, Arthur was a bank manager and John Suffield tolerated their union enough to allow Mabel to set sail in March, to be with her betrothed.

Mabel was an unusual young woman, marrying for love at a time when that was not the norm in England, and was educated in German, Latin, French, art and piano, in spite of her father John's bankruptcy. John himself was a travelling salesman for Jeyes disinfectant, but he was fiercely proud of the drapery business his family had once owned, and of their strong Midlands' heritage. In fact, that was one of the reasons he disliked Arthur's marriage to Mabel. Although to the onlooker the Tolkiens and Suffields seemed of similar social standing, both middle-class former owners of craft businesses fallen on hard times, John disliked the Tolkiens for what he saw as their lack of heritage, perceiving them as 'mere German immigrants, English by only a few generations!'[2] Nonetheless, perhaps motivated by the hope of a better life for his daughter overseas, he bade her farewell with his blessing.

After the three-week voyage, Mabel landed in Cape Town harbour, and was greeted by a moustachioed gentlemen, clad in a dandy-style white suit, and peering through the crowd in nervously, frantic to catch a glimpse of his dear 'Mab' after so long apart. The couple were wed on 16 April 1891 in Cape Town Cathedral, and honeymooned at a hotel in Sea Point, before braving the several hundred mile journey to their home in Bloemfontein.

As the capital of the Orange Free State, perhaps Bloemfontein had sounded more fanciful to Mabel in Arthur's letters, for when she arrived there she – a Birmingham city girl through-and-through – was distinctly unimpressed. To her it seemed the capital city had very little capital and even less to do. The 45-year-old settlement, with less than a handful of clubs, a single library, a single hospital, and a marketplace predominantly taken over by the wool bales that were the state's main trade, were not to Mabel's tastes. Moreover, there was little greenery; in letters to her family, Mabel described the only park as a few willows by some scant water and the town as a whole as a wilderness.[3]

However disagreeable she found the place, she could see that Arthur was happy here, and thoroughly in love with his work. Although his position as an *uitlander* (outsider: only permitted to work there by a government decree) was insecure, he learned Dutch in his free time and networked extensively to shore up his position. In short, a return visit home seemed a long way away, which worried Mabel. But their home, Bank House, was beautiful, with a garden and a balcony, and staff, and when he wasn't working she and Arthur spent their time playing against each other at golf and tennis, and reading aloud. It was into this happy home that John Ronald Reuel Tolkien was born on 3 January, 1892.

Although both John Ronald and Mabel were hail and healthy, the boy's birth was something of a drama. In a letter to his mother on 4 January, Arthur relays that when they first called for a Dr Strollreither, he decided it was a false alarm and told the nurse to go home for two weeks! Fortunately, Arthur was more sensitive to his wife's condition and called the doctor back later in the evening, when he acquiesced that she was in fact in labour. The doctor stayed from around eight until after midnight, when he and Arthur shared a whisky to toast John Ronald's health.

The same letter reveals some of the history behind the J.R.Rs of the famous author's name. John and Reuel were Arthur's choices and favourites (John being his father's name and Reuel his own middle name), but Mabel's favourite was Ronald. Ronald ended up being the name his parents and later his wife knew him by, through some close friends called him John Ronald, and later names he went by included Tollers and J.R.R.T. In fact, he said on more than one occasion that Ronald 'did not feel like his real name'.[4]

It is perhaps, with this lifelong precedent, valid to draw the conclusion that the recurring theme of multiple names in Tolkien's Middle-Earth works had some personal significance. Stoor hobbits and Dwarves go by multiple names: their common parlance names (e.g. Sméagol and Déagol) and their secret, true Westron names (Trahald and Mahald). In one of the many parallels drawn between Dwarves and Stoor hobbits, Dwarves also have secret names in their language, 'Khuzdul', which are unknown to non-Dwarves.[5] More specifically, names in Middle-Earth carry a tremendous amount of personal weight, Sméagol famously being able to reclaim some of his lost agency and sanity when Frodo addresses him as Sméagol, rather than Gollum: the name conferred upon him once he lost himself to the One Ring. Similarly, Gríma Wormtongue finds the strength to rebel against Saruman when Saruman calls him 'Worm' in public as a final insult. In a reverse of this, Bilbo Baggins is able to defeat the matriarch of the spiders of Mirkwood by naming her 'Attercop' (an old English word for an old spider). These meditations on personhood, identity and strength through names that permeate Tolkien's works provide a fascinating insight into Tolkien's own identity. He was a man who seemed amphibious: living half in this world and half in his own, perhaps only able to grasp that rich vein of creativity through not feeling truly 'named' in reality.

John Ronald was raised in a household that was somewhat unusual for the colonial Boer town. Many of the house staff were Black natives or people from other non-White communities, and Mabel objected strongly to the Boer oppression of the native population and headed her household with kindliness and friendship to all her staff (a stark contrast to her own family's narrow view of what even constituted Englishness). One of the staff who felt particularly close to the Tolkiens was a Black house servant named Isaak, who can be seen in the photograph of baby John Ronald and his parents at his christening, alongside a maid whose name has unfortunately not been recorded. Isaak was a spirited man and a great help to the Tolkien family, though is perhaps best remembered for causing a bizarre incident in baby Ronald's life.

Confident in the trust of his employers, one day Isaak took the infant Ronald with him to his kraal to show off this White baby to his friends and neighbours. Upon returning, he found the house – in particular Mabel – in a state of panic and dismay. Unfortunately, as Isaak had not told the Tolkiens his plan, they had expected their baby to be in the shade of the house in midday and saw no sign of him, and – as there were wolves, jackals and lions that posed a very real threat to infants in the area – feared the worst.[6] But Isaak safely returned the baby to his anxious parents, and continued to work for the family (such actions were considered grounds for immediate dismissal in the Boer culture), remaining so close to the family that years later he named his first-born son Isaak Mister Tolkien Victor, after Arthur and Queen Victoria.

Drama followed the young John Ronald, in a climate he didn't take to and with wildlife as majestic as it was dangerous surrounding him, leaving him sickly and his mother alternately anxious and longing for home. The neighbours kept pet monkeys. The noise was enough but one day they scaled the wall separating the two homes and broke into Bank House, shredding three of baby Ronald's pinafores. The woodshed – well stocked for the cold, damp winters – provided a perfect habitat for snakes. And worst of all, when he was just learning to walk, John Ronald, taking tentative steps in his own garden, tripped on a tarantula. The tarantula, unaware that the stumbling burbling thing dressed all in white meant it no harm, bit. Decades later, Tolkien recalled running senselessly around the garden, terrified and boiling hot, but completely unaware of what he was running for or from. Fortunately, his nurse recognised something was very wrong and picked him up, finding the bite and quickly sucking out the poison. He fondly recalled in later life to his friend and former student W.H. Auden that, in spite of the incident, '[he did] not dislike spiders particularly, and [had] no urge to kill them'.[7]

In spite of this, many scholars and fans have sought to draw a connection between this childhood incident and Ungoliant, the dark, primordial entity that 'took shape as a spider of monstrous form'.[8] This eternally ravenous entity is both the only being to make the evil Melkor scream in fear in *The Silmarillion* and the matriarch from whom all the other giant spiders in Middle-Earth are descended. However, it should be noted that Ungoliant, her daughter Shelob, and Attercop and her brood in Mirkwood have more in common in behaviour and name etymology with enlarged English spiders than they do tarantulas, and more symbolic resonance with Arachne and the titular *Black Spider* of Gotthelf's seminal 1842 work. (Though Ungoliant, unlike Arachne and Christine, has agency in her form, she is an incomprehensible being that chooses to be a spider, rather than a human woman having the transformation forced upon her.)

But these webs of intrigue are far in toddler John Ronald's future. Of course, arachnid injuries notwithstanding, there were good times too. Arthur planted a small grove in the garden, where Ronald would watch him tend to his cedars, cypresses and firs in the morning and afternoon. In the heat of the day, Ronald would be taken inside, for the hot weather made him very ill. To offer some protection, Mabel dressed him in all white at all times to reflect some of the heat. This gave young Ronald a whimsical appearance, as Mabel describes in a letter to her mother-in-law, 'Baby does look such a fairy when he's very much dressed up in white frills,' adding, 'when he's very much undressed I think he looks more of an elf still.'[9]

Although the household was usually harmonious, there was an ever-growing rift between Arthur and Mabel, as she longed for their visit home (which could be taken in about a year's time) and he kept finding reasons to postpone it. Even though his health did not like the arid veldt, Mabel could see that his temperament suited the climate, and worried privately that he might become too attached to his life in South Africa, but promised her family that she would not let him delay their trip too long. However, although their return visit did end up postponed, it was for happy reasons: Mabel was pregnant once again. Hilary Arthur Reuel was born on 17 February 1894.

Although Hilary took after his father in seeming perfectly at peace in the heat, Ronald was becoming more and more sickly. This was not helped by extreme conditions even for Bloemfontein that year: the summer was fiercely hot, and there was a severe drought. In spite of this, the harvest prevailed, only to be utterly destroyed by a swarm of locusts. Ronald, feverish from teething, worried Mabel so much that she called upon the doctor almost daily, and Mabel and her nurses – managing a sickly toddler and a newborn – were completely exhausted.

Arthur could see something had to be done, but his duties at the bank were critical, and deep in his heart, he truly loved life in Bloemfontein. Even that year, with the tumult and stress both outside and inside his home, he wrote to his father that he was considering permanently settling in South Africa, fully believing he would thrive there.[10] This is not to say that he was unaware or unsympathetic to his wife and child's needs. Recognising that, even if they could not return to England for a spell, Mabel and Ronald certainly could not stay in Bloemfontein. So it was that Mabel took the two boys on the long train journey to the coast near Cape Town. Ronald enjoyed the trip, and even remembered both the 'endless' train journey and 'bathing in the Indian Ocean' into adulthood.[11]

The holiday made things clear even to Arthur: Ronald needed to be out of the heat, and Mabel needed that visit to England. So upon their return he paid for Mabel and the boys to voyage to England on the SS *Guelph* in April 1895, accompanied by a nurse. However, despite being extremely close to his family, Arthur could not travel with them. Business at the bank was urgent and unavoidable; there were critical railway scheme dealings Arthur needed to manage. Additionally, he likely could not afford the leave: time away would be on half-pay and the cost of the voyage itself had set him back considerably. Nonetheless, he promised he would follow on as soon as he could, and helped Mabel and the boys prepare for the trip in any way he could, even small ways such a painting *A. R. Tolkien* on their cabin trunk. This small gesture would become Ronald's first and only memory of his father.

But new experiences for the boys, and a long-awaited homecoming for Mabel, awaited. After the three-week voyage, her younger sister Jane met them at Southampton, and the group travelled to Birmingham, where they stayed with Mabel's parents. John Suffield proved to be a loving grandfather, boisterous and always cracking jokes and making puns to entertain the boys, and his wife was kind and understanding of Mabel's difficult situation. The Suffields' house was tiny in comparison to Bank House, which deeply confused young Ronald, who often wondered where the balcony of Bank House had gone,[12] being too young to understand at first that this was a different place.

The house was smaller and also more crowded with relatives, another novel experience for Ronald. Mabel's brother and sister, Willie and Jane, still lived at home, and there was a lodger: an insurance clerk who played the banjo, which Ronald found rather marvellous, making him wish for a banjo of his own. However, he kept this desire to himself, as the family found the lodger 'common', and were not happy when Jane later became engaged to him.

But life in the house on Ashfield Road was a lot of fun for the boys, and Ronald was now healthy. Spring in Birmingham became summer, and summer became autumn. Still there was no sign of Arthur. Every time Mabel wrote to him he had another reason to keep him at his desk, though he missed them dearly. And in November Mabel received even worse news: Arthur had contracted rheumatic fever. He would be unable to travel, let alone face winter in England. He had to rest up and regain his strength.

For Hilary and Ronald, too young to comprehend the potential severity of this news, this meant another unexpected delight: Christmas in England with their relatives. Ronald was enamoured with the Christmas tree, a real fir, unlike the rather depressing wilting eucalyptus Arthur had proudly presented the previous year, and both children enjoyed being spoiled by a large and welcoming family who had not met them before.

But, of course, Mabel was anxious. By the time she had received the news that Arthur was ill he had been in recovery, yet by January he was still sick. Unable to stand the sense of powerlessness, Mabel decided she must return to Bloemfontein to care for him. She made the arrangements, and explained to the children that they were going to see their father again. Ecstatic, Ronald dictated a letter to his nurse, delighted at the prospect of seeing his father again after so long away, excitedly telling him how much he and his baby brother had grown, and how much walking he was doing.[13]

The letter is dated 14 February 1896. It was never sent, for a telegram arrived. Arthur Tolkien had suffered severe haemorrhaging as a result of complications of his rheumatic fever, and Mabel was to 'expect the worst'. Although the full account of his death would only reach Mabel after he was buried, Arthur Tolkien had died the day after Ronald's letter was penned.

Chapter 2

The Ogres at Sarehole

What was Mabel to do? She was a young widow, with scarcely enough resources to provide for both of her boys. Arthur's job certainly could have provided comfortable wealth in the future, but at the time of his death he was not terribly well off. His life in Bloemfontein had been oxymoronic and precarious; although Bank House was beautiful and they had maintained a full service staff, that was to be expected of the Bank of Africa manager and as such maintaining the lifestyle had taken up most of his salary. The majority of his remaining finances were invested in the Bonanza Mines, paying to Mabel a dividend of 30 shillings a week (approximately £170.20 in real terms today).[1]

She had to think fast, and work out a way to provide for her boys whilst still grieving her husband. Living in the already-crowded Suffield town house was not an option; although they had been lodged there for almost a year as guests, space was already at a premium and the boys were growing fast and more boisterous. She had to come up with a long-term plan. The boys' education was foremost in her mind. She had already decided that they were to sit the entrance exam for their late father's *alma mata*, Birmingham's King Edward's School. This was the best grammar school in the area at the time and would hopefully give them the best start in life. But what of their education up until then? After all, that was a few years away. Mabel decided that she would teach her boys until they were old enough for King Edward's, but in the meantime, she had to find a new place to live.

In those early post-Arthur days, still in their grandparents' house on Ashfield Road, Ronald and Hilary, now fatherless, gravitated to other adults in their lives. There was Aunt Grace (or 'Aunt Gracie' as Ronald called her in his unsent letter to his father), Arthur's younger sister, who liked to tell the children grand stories about how the Tolkiens got their name and came to England. And there was John Benjamin Tolkien, John Ronald's paternal grandfather, an 89-year-old gentleman, and the last of the Tolkiens to be a clock- and piano-maker, who lived just up the road from the Suffields. The boys were sometimes taken to visit him, but he was a frail and sensitive man, and outliving his son thoroughly broke him, and he passed away not six months after Arthur.

Perhaps the figure who loomed largest in the hearts and minds of Ronald and Hilary was their maternal grandfather, John Suffield. He was a boisterous and jovial man, 63 years old and determined to live to see his hundredth birthday. A favourite party trick of his was to draw around a sixpence with a fine-nibbed pen and write the entire Lord's Prayer in copperplate inside the circle.[2] He would explain to the boys that the Suffields had been engravers historically, and that they had their own coat of arms, bestowed upon them by King William IV for their commendable work, and that Lord Suffield was a distant relative (he was not).

John Suffield was not the only relative fond of telling tall tales of ancestry. On the Tolkien side, Aunt Gracie had a similarly extensive and entirely unsourced mythic creation for the Tolkien name and line. According to her, the 'von Hohenzollerns' as they once were (as they were from the Holy Roman Empire's Hohenzollern district), became the *Tollkühns* (literally: foolhardy) because one George von Hohenzollern captured the Turkish sultan's standard in an unofficial raid for Archduke Ferdinand during the Siege of Vienna in 1529. From there the *Tollkühns* allegedly intermarried into French nobility, becoming the *du Téméraire*s, before fleeing the guillotine by coming to England, and, upon arrival, changing their name to Tolkien.[3] There was a conflicting and more believable version of events, where the Tolkiens came to England in 1756 to escape their lands being seized during the Prussian invasion of Saxony, but that was not the one that Gracie told.

Although these sorts of fanciful ancestral tales were at the time not uncommon in the English middle classes, these struck a particular chord with Ronald, who recounted some of Gracie's tales (and especially the one of the capture of the Turkish standard) throughout his life.

However fond young Ronald was of his Aunt Gracie and her invented histories, it was to the Suffields he felt the closest kinship, describing himself as 'a Suffield by tastes, talents and upbringing' as an adult.[4] Through digging into their family history, he found out they had deep roots in Evesham, Worcestershire, and this gave him a sense of belonging and history he craved, raised as he was in a culture where mythic history was everything, at a time when he was suddenly unable to return to the land of his birth.

It is difficult to learn of Tolkien's early childhood, with these eccentric relatives who told tall tales and practised detailed, pensive crafts, and not think of the Hobbits of the Shire, in particular the Baggins and Tooks. In *The Lord of the Rings*, Frodo starts the story as the ward of his elderly but unusually vivacious uncle Bilbo Baggins, his parents having drowned when he was young. Bilbo Baggins is a jolly storyteller and poet, and both Bilbo and Frodo are descendants of Bandobras Took, a famous Hobbiton folk hero who defended the Shire from goblins in the Battle of Greenfields by knocking the goblin king Golfimbul's head off with a club, winning the battle and inadvertently inventing golf at the same time. This is not to say that Frodo or Bilbo are direct allegorical counterparts to Ronald and John – far from it – but that these parallels Ronald lavished on his life's works with his own early childhood indicate how important this sense of family and history was to him. In the books, the Shire represents an ideal home, which the characters long for and must fight to preserve. In this context, it is clear why Tolkien felt so very close to his Suffield family, as their mannerisms and sense of community found their way into his fantasy world decades later.

Something else that found its way into Tolkien's created world and his heart was the home Mabel found for them in the summer of 1896, 5 Gracewell in Sarehole. Although it was only about a mile away from the hustle and bustle of Birmingham, the little Worcestershire (later Warwickshire) village of Sarehole was a small rural community, rich with greenery and agriculture that the boys fell in love with. It was almost an anachronism for the time; nothing was motorised, horses and carts were the only vehicles on the roads, and it was populated largely by farm labourers as opposed to factory workers. Humphrey Carpenter (Tolkien's only official biographer) put it best when he said, 'Just at the age when his imagination was opening out, [Tolkien] found himself in the heart of the English countryside.'5

Sarehole would live on forever in both Hilary and Ronald's hearts. From the age of two-and-a-half, Hilary could be found traipsing after his brother as they played by the stream-like River Cole, or chased the swans in the large pond, or investigated the mill. The miller's son, a stern and sharp-featured man who would shout at the children if he caught them by the mill, was nicknamed by Ronald the White Ogre, for the white dust on his person from his milling. Unbeknownst to the miller's son, the White Ogre also had a counterpart, the Black Ogre, a dark-bearded farmer who once chased Ronald for stealing mushrooms. Other characters that stuck with the boys included a toothless older lady who they used to buy sweets from, and the local children, who they became friends with, after first receiving some teasing. The local working-class country children found the boys' middle-class aesthetics funny: their long hair, pinafores and accents – and took to jokingly calling them 'wenches'.[6]

In his adage, Hilary Tolkien looked back on his and his brother's shenanigans fondly.

> 'We spent lovely summers just picking flowers and trespassing. The Black Ogre used to take people's shoes and stockings from the bank where they'd left them to paddle, and run away with them, make them go and ask for them. Then he'd thrash them! The White Ogre wasn't quite so bad. But in order to get to the place where we used to blackberry... we had to go through the white one's land, and he didn't like us very much... My mother got us lunch to have in this lovely place, but when she arrived she made a deep voice, and we both ran!'[7]

Whereas Hilary was fond of he and his brother's high jinks, what lasted in Ronald's memory was the place itself. In later life, he spoke of an old mill (which he believed ground corn), a large swan-filled pond, a flower-cloaked dell, old-fashioned houses and a second mill by a small stream.[8] It should be noted that the White Ogre's nickname was more pertinent than Ronald realised; his mill did not 'really grind corn', it had in the past, but had now been modified to grind bone for manure production,[9] adding a soupçon of macabre to Ronald's idyllic childhood memories.

There are clear, direct and intentional parallels in Tolkien's creation of the Shire and the mannerisms of Hobbits, with his time in Sarehole, and the place itself. Firstly, there is the hobbit habit of close friendships between two male relatives who enjoy exploring the countryside together, the most famous pair of course being the cousins Merry and Pippin of the Fellowship of the Ring, but Sméagol and Déagol's friendship also follows this pattern. Frodo Baggins and Samwise Gamgee are the exception to this rule as they are not related, Sam being Frodo's employee, but their relationship takes inspiration from other sources later in Tolkien's life. However, Samwise does owe his names to Tolkien's time in Sarehole, where Ronald picked up the colloquial term for cotton wool – gamgee tissue – after local household name Dr Samson Gamgee who invented a form of cotton wool surgical dressing.

Frodo as a child being chased by Farmer Maggot for stealing mushrooms is another direct parallel, but Farmer Maggot's later bravery and help when Frodo and his friends need to flee from the Black Riders seems to be an adult Ronald's admission that maybe the Black Ogre was not the villain his childhood imagination made him out to be. In contrast, memories of Ronald and Hilary spending their days picking flowers were used to create a subversion of innocence in Sméagol's story of losing himself to the One Ring. Sméagol and his dear friend and cousin Déagol spend Sméagol's birthday on an outing picking flowers, fishing and digging on the riverbank, until Déagol finds the One Ring upon being dragged into the water, and his cousin covets it, and is affected by its corruptive power enough to murder his best friend for it. Tolkien drew on a strong memory of childhood innocence to emphasise the horrific effect of the Ring's influence and Sméagol's corruption into Gollum.

Additionally, the place of Sarehole itself was a direct influence in the creation of the Shire. Tolkien himself repeatedly identified the Shire as akin to Sarehole, describing how coming from the aridity of South Africa to the trees and rivers of the Warwickshire Midlands at such a crucial age had a profound effect on him.[10] The Shire reflects what Duriez called Tolkien's 'heart-home',[11] a place that he carried with him and cherished throughout his life, and poured into his work for the world to see.

Of course, when they weren't 'picking flowers and trespassing', as Hilary said, there were lessons. Mabel's curriculum was varied: English, Latin, French, drawing, painting, botany, piano, and (no doubt to John Suffield's great delight) calligraphy. Some of these Ronald took to like a duck to water, others he did not. Unfortunately, despite being cut from the cloth of guillotine-dodging piano-makers, he could not play, despite Mabel's best efforts. However, botany proved a much more successful area of study for Ronald. He and Hilary were already interested enough in plants in general, but Ronald had a fascination and love of trees that would last his whole life. This led to him excelling at botany, but he also just enjoyed the presence of trees, not just for climbing, but for sitting by and talking to also. He was heartbroken when a neighbour cut down a willow, '[It was] hanging over the mill-pool and I learned to climb it. It belonged to a butcher... I think. One day they cut it down. They didn't do anything with it: the log just lay there. I never forgot that,' he recalled as an adult.[12] It is possible that Old Man Willow, the implied-Huorn (a race of sentient trees in Middle-Earth) on the banks of the Withywindle, that entraps and nearly kills Merry and Pippin in *Lord of the Rings*, is a form of vengeance for the senselessly felled willow of Tolkien's childhood. Notably, although Old Man Willow is dangerous, it is left intentionally ambiguous as to whether or not he is malicious, or merely angry at creatures who would cut him down, as he is protected by Tom Bombadil, a forest guardian.

But aside from botany there was another subject Ronald excelled at: Latin, which Mabel astutely recognised as a flair for and love of languages in general, and so began to teach him the rules of Latin and English, which he was extremely enthused by, as well as French, which he liked far less. However, he was also extremely fond of dialect English, and learned much of it from the country boys he and Hilary befriended, including 'pikelet' (crumpet), 'miskin' (dustbin) and of course 'gamgee' (cotton wool) being some of his favourites.[13] This would become a lifelong passion: for Ronald's specialty as an Oxford professor was Midlands dialect English. From childhood, Ronald was a passionate reader and speaker, and completely fascinated with language as a whole, while also being a talented artist and calligrapher.

His tastes in book were quite particular. He did not like the popular boys' favourite of the time *Treasure Island*, or any Hans Christian Anderson fairy tales, and was only mildly entertained by *Alice In Wonderland*. But he did love Arthurian legends, and Andrew Lang's Fairy books, but there were three books that left a notable impression on him, inspiring themes and details in his works for years to come.

The first were 'Red Indian' tales, works that were in no way accurate or fair representations of the Indigenous Peoples of America, but rather pulpy nonsense capitalising on the Western fascination with the 'exotic' and their creation of a 'savage' which they 'bravely' opposed. Nonetheless, these tales did give young Ronald a desire to use, and fascination with, bows and arrows. This fascination would come to fruition in the creation of Elven archers and the Mannish hero, Bard the Bowman, in adulthood.

The second were the *Princess Irene* books by George Macdonald. These books, which featured malicious oddly shaped goblins dwelling under mountains, hugely influenced Tolkien's depiction of goblins, most notably in *The Hobbit*, which is aimed at younger children in the same way Macdonald's books were. Although the citizens of Goblin-town did not share Princess Irene's foes' weakness of soft feet, they do suffer physical maladies from living underground, live under mountains, and have a chaotic energy just like Macdonald's ragtag creations.

Finally, there was the story at the end of Lang's *Red Fairy Book*: a retelling of the slaying of Fafnir the dragon by the hero Sigurd. He read it over and over and became thoroughly fascinated with dragons. 'I desired dragons with a profound desire.'[14] he later recalled. This inspired him to write what seems to be his first ever fiction story, one about a large dragon. No record of it has survived, and Ronald, philologist through-and-through, can remember only one detail from it, a linguistic one: that his mother corrected his title for the dragon from 'green great dragon' to 'great green dragon'.[15] This great green dragon's story may have been lost to time and perhaps a young author with a short attention span, but he is the ancestor of some of the greatest dragons in fiction. The dragons of Middle-Earth, from Smaug the Terrible of *The Hobbit* to the almost incomprehensibly huge Ancalagon the Black of *The Silmarillion*, all have an archaic mythic quality to them; they are all named, sentient, and as intelligent as they are powerful. Even in the historic-feeling Middle-Earth they feel great and ageless, relics of a bygone time not fully documented by Tolkien or any of his in-universe scholars. This is because they all take inspiration from Scandinavian folk tales and Norse mythology, and that passion started with Lang's retelling of the slaying of Fafnir.

These skills and passions forged in Sarehole would be lifelong, but there was one other less pleasant thing which started here that was sadly just as chronic. Ronald began to have a recurring dream that he was drowning, which he humorously called his 'Atlantis complex' in adulthood.[16] The specific dream Ronald had was of a green wave that subsumed the land. Duriez' interpretation of the impact of Tolkien's dream was that this was part of the inspiration for the Fall of Númenor as counted in *The Silmarillion*,[17] his own version of an Atlantis, Gilgamesh or Noah's Ark-style flood story, the land sunk due to the hubris and blasphemous practices of its people, holds water. Additionally, it is possible that this dream and fear, started in Ronald's early childhood, connects it to the drowning death of Frodo's parents prior to the events of *The Lord of the Rings*, and the community-wide fear Shire hobbits have of large bodies of water.

The final and perhaps most seismic event in young Ronald's life at this time concerned faith. His family were staunch Anglican Christians, and Mabel had always observed, and raised the boys as such, but that was about to change. To understand this, we must first travel back to Mabel leaving her home for Arthur and Bloemfontein. She was particularly close to her sisters; her younger sister Jane helped ferry love letters between her and Arthur prior to their betrothal, and her older sister May was one of her most frequent correspondents once she had left. In fact, May and her husband, Walter Incledon, later joined Mabel in Bloemfontein. Walter had professional interests in the gold and diamond mines, but May's impact on and friendship with her sister at that time cannot be overstated. Arthur was away for some weeks with bank dealings, the summer was bitterly cold, and Mabel was struggling to keep her newborn baby warm. The sisters knitted clothes for baby Ronald by the fire, and weathered the severe climate and isolation together. May, a dear and lifelong friend to Mabel in her times of need, always steadfast and there for her sister through thick and thin, plays a pivotal role at this point.

The next chapter of the Tolkiens' life is tricky to capture. The events are known, but the reasons behind them are not, because those who can remember it were either children at the time or passed away before it became a matter of public interest, but one of the most important, and oft-overlooked, elements of this tale is the deep connection between these two women. It is unclear whom suggested it to whom, but at this moment in their lives these sisters made a dramatic change, one which shook their lives and family to the core and hugely impacted the morality and spirituality of one of the most influential pieces of fiction in the Western fantasy canon: they changed religion.

May Incledon had now moved back to England, with her own young children (two daughters) in tow, and Walter was to follow after. It was at this time May (separated from her husband for the first time since marriage and under the exact circumstances with which her younger sister became a widow) and Mabel (widowed, grieving, and raising and educating her two boys on a pauper's income) reunited in person. From here, the details of what these women thought, the discussions they had with one another, are lost to history and the memories of children. It is to Hilary's sharp memory of a certain Sunday we can attribute the first practical change. Every Sunday, they had walked the well-worn route to the local Anglican church. Now, they took a different route, and went to a different church: the Roman Catholic church.

Within both the Suffields and the Tolkiens there was uproar. Most of the Tolkiens were Baptists, and the Suffields were a mix of Anglicans, Methodists and Unitarians. The small but critical amount of financial help Mabel had been receiving from her family was cut. Her only support networks after the death of Arthur; her family and her local Anglican church community, ostracised her. But she and May stayed firm, and found roots in their local Catholic community, and clearly profound sustenance from their faith, because they both became very devout. But for May this could not last. Walter was furious. Upon his return from South Africa, he forbade May from practising her faith, or even so much as *entering* a Catholic church ever again. He considered himself a pillar of the local Anglican community (an interesting thought considering he had been away from it for years to seek his fortune in gold and diamonds but, nonetheless, this was his perception of himself) and he used this belief to suppress his wife's religious freedom. May had no choice but to comply, and began practising Anglican Christianity once more in spite of her own beliefs. Fortunately, she did eventually find solace by incorporating spiritualism into her faith, which was frowned upon, but although Walter did not approve she had not renounced Anglican Christianity and so could practise as she wished.

But for now, May could only manage a small victory. Walter had been providing a small amount of financial help to Mabel, but now that was abruptly cut off. However, where the rest of Mabel's family had turned their backs on her, the Incledons did not, no doubt due to May. Although Walter no longer financially contributed towards Mabel's household, Mabel and her boys were frequent visitors, and vice versa, providing Ronald and Hilary with much-needed friendships and playmates in their cousins Mary and Marjorie.

Mabel's faith and the sacrifices she made for it had a profound effect on Tolkien. Ronald remained a devout Catholic his entire life, and religious themes are present – if subtly cloaked – in Middle-Earth. Tolkien crafted the world as a mythic past for our world, in particular England, and as such, although there are many 'gods' in his pantheon (who are worshipped as such by the Elves, Men and Dwarves), they are intended to be mere angels of the Catholic god, here called Eru Ilúvatar.

As contradictory as it might outwardly appear for a deeply religious man to write characters living in our world worshipping in a way that is not congruent with his own faith, in spite of his God being a presence in that world, much of Tolkien's personal faith was intricately woven with his belief in a 'mythic truth' that the word and intention of his Catholic god could be found in other forms through different cultures' myths and practices. Wider ramifications of this are explored in later chapters, but suffice to say that his unique, and more accepting version of faith was not entirely welcomed by others.

For example, after the publication of *The Lord of the Rings*, a Mr Peter Hastings, owner of a Catholic bookshop in Oxford, wrote to Tolkien to protest that Elves were reincarnated, disgruntled as

'God has not used that device in any of the creations of which we have knowledge... because a sub-creator, when dealing with the relations between creator and created, should use those channels which he knows the creator to have used already.'[18]

As strange as it might seem to us to lay such a complaint at one of the foundational figures of adult fantasy fiction in the West, Tolkien's drafted reply does give us some insight into his thought process in relation to his faith.

'Liberation "from the channels the creator is known to have used already" is the fundamental function of "sub-creation", a tribute to the infinity of His potential variety... I am not a metaphysician; but I should have thought it a curious metaphysic – there is not one but many, indeed potentially innumerable ones – that declared the channels known (in such a finite corner as we have any inkling of) to have been used, are the only possible ones, or efficacious, or possibly acceptable to and by Him!'[19]

In fact, within this correspondence we see a glimpse of Tolkien's views and feelings towards his Protestant family, as he disputes Mr Hastings' claim that Tom Bombadil is Eru or an avatar of him (which Mr Hastings finds blasphemous). Tolkien's response: 'I really do think you are being too serious, besides missing the point… You rather remind me of a Protestant relation who to me objected to the (modern) Catholic habit of calling priests Father, because the name father belonged only to the First Person.'[20]

Indeed, Tolkien's flexible and adaptable faith seems to have been forged in opposition to what his family put Mabel through. Ronald went from having a supportive and welcoming extended family to seeing his mother being made a pariah in a few short weeks, when he was young enough not to fully understand why, but old enough to never forget. John Suffield, the jolly grandfather who had welcomed them into his home when they first returned to England, who had supported his daughter through the death of her husband, who *himself* had converted from Methodism to Unitarianism in his own lifetime, was now wrathful, seeing his daughters' 'papism' as a betrayal. His kindly aunt May, one of the few figures who had journeyed with him nearly his whole life, over two continents, was not allowed to come to the church she had chosen. And his mother, whom he loved dearly, who did her level best to provide love and support for him and Hilary, was becoming sick with stress at his family's hand.

In later life, Tolkien described his childhood as 'dreadful sufferings'.[21] Although he was too young to remember the death of his father, Mabel's persecution was burned into his mind. There are ghosts of Mabel's influence throughout both *The Hobbit* and *The Lord of the Rings*, but this aspect of her life, the isolation she faced whilst raising her boys, is perhaps directly reflected through Bilbo Baggins in *The Lord of the Rings*. Prior to the events of *The Hobbit*, Bilbo is considered an upstanding gentleman of leisure within Hobbiton, but through his 'adventure' he witnesses kidnapping, imprisonment, war, and the death of his close friend (the Dwarven King Thorin Oakenshield) and Thorin's young nephews. Upon returning home almost a year later, he finds his neighbours selling his furniture, and himself ostracised for now having an adventurous spirit and being welcoming to travelling Dwarves. By the time of *The Lord of the Rings*, sixty years have passed and Bilbo is being driven slowly mad by Ring Sickness, is by turns celebrated by his community and ostracised by his family, and – crucially – is raising young Frodo Baggins, his own orphaned nephew.

In seeing the parallels between Bilbo and Mabel, there is something of a grim triumph to Tolkien's arc for Bilbo. After being separated from the

Ring, he is able to visit his Dwarven and Elven friends one last time, and know of the defeat of the Dark Lord Sauron, welcome his ward safely home, and then sail West (essentially voyaging to paradise without dying). Bilbo gets to be lauded for his achievements, and to live to see the child he raised become a young man. Mabel did not.

Aside from the metaphorical dark clouds on the horizon for Mabel and her boys, there were literal ones, for life at Sarehole could not continue forever. Ronald was at schooling age, and after first sitting King Edward's entrance exam in 1899 (and then passing it in 1900), the family had to find lodging back in the industrial heart of Birmingham once again. Fortunately, a more understanding uncle on the Tolkien side happily arranged with Mabel that he should pay Ronald's fees (£12.00 per year; £1,275.00 in real terms today),[22] but the question of accommodation still remained. All three of them loved Sarehole so, and for the first few weeks of term they tried to make the best of it, Ronald walking almost 4 miles to school every day (for the family could not afford train or tram fare for the whole of such a long journey), but obviously this was untenable. Eventually, Mabel managed to find a place that was within her meagre budget, closer to the centre and on the tramway to make Ronald's life a little easier.

In the tail-end of 1900, almost perfectly dovetailing with the end of the Victorian era a year later, Mabel, Ronald and Hilary Tolkien moved into a little rented house in Moseley, closing the four-year long chapter of their life in Sarehole.

Who better to close out this chapter – both literally and metaphorically – than Tolkien himself, writing on Sarehole in his adage:

'Four years, but the longest-seeming and most formative part of my life.'[23]

Chapter 3

City Languages and Warring Trees

Despite the admittedly far less brutal commute, Ronald was still struggling in his new school and away from the peace and joy of his heart-home. Moseley was more industrial, to Ronald's eyes more horrible, and he hated having to leave Sarehole behind. School, overcrowded and noisy, and away from his brother, was not much better. Ronald valued peace and quiet, missed the countryside and his beloved trees, and struggled to find his feet. King Edward's student population had ballooned since its founding by Edward VI to become a Birmingham institution, with branches throughout the city, including the slums, to provide the highest-rated education in the city to boys from a plethora of backgrounds. But Ronald, stationed in the main site, was in a cramped, noisy and crowded building, at once ancient and pulsing with life. One can only imagine how disorienting it must have been to arrive to that after the serenity of home schooling in a nigh-on pre-Industrial village.

Throughout much of Ronald's first term he was absent with illness. The city air and the cramped school conditions, not to mention the stress from a home life where his mother (and by extension him and his brother) were still pariahs in a once-welcoming family, wreaked havoc on his health.

Nonetheless, Ronald was a plucky and determined child to say the least. With Mabel's help, he recovered as quickly and as best he could, and threw himself into school life, eventually learning to love the hustle and bustle of his peers, even if he was still not achieving all he could academically. Mabel could clearly see he was a gifted child, but for some reason King Edward's was not bringing that out of him.

The Tolkiens' tumultuous home life was certainly not helping. Scarcely after they'd moved to Moseley, they were forced to move again, as the house they rented was set to be demolished to make room for a fire station. But their time in King's Heath was not all doom and gloom; in fact, it was the start of what was to become one of Ronald's lifelong passions. Close to the station as they were, Ronald could look out at the embankment (which – much to his delight – was thick with wild flowers), watch the trains go by, and on the side of many of the coal freighters, he saw words which ignited his imagination. *Blaen-Rhondda, Maerdy, Nantyglo, Tredegar*[1]... this was Tolkien's first encounter with Welsh. A later holiday confirmed to him that thrill he felt upon first reading the language: he was fascinated by its antiquity for a living language, and very much wanted to study it. However, all the books he could find on the subject were incomprehensible to a boy not yet in double figures. He needed a foothold into the language, and little did he know that one was just around the corner.

With Ronald struggling at school, and the neighbourhood they found themselves in dull and unimaginative, Mabel sought other options. She found a terraced house to let by King's Heath Station, very close to her parents, but that was not her primary reason for the move. It was also near to St Dunstan's Catholic Church. However, that community and support Mabel sought for herself and her family was not fully provided at St Dunstan's. It was not as welcoming a faith experience as Mabel had hoped. So once again, one Sunday, the boys had to make a long and unusual trek to a different church.

Where Mabel now took the boys to worship was the Birmingham Oratory, situated in Edgbaston. And here, finally, Mabel found what she had been looking for since perhaps before Arthur even passed away: a stable, supportive community and a place and style of worship that felt like home. Perhaps this was because the Oratory was founded by John Henry Newman, then a recent convert himself, who had only passed away twelve years prior to Mabel and family joining the congregation in 1902, so several of his acolytes were still working there, creating a more welcome environment for converts.

With the grounding point of her life now Birmingham Oratory, Mabel took stock of her lot. Her boys weren't demonstrating the academic prowess she knew they were capable of at King Edward's. Although she was physically close to her family, they remained emotionally distant to her. And fees and the trek to worship just kept adding up and up... so Mabel made the decision to move her family one last time. Closer to the Oratory, there was a Catholic grammar school – St Philip's – which had affordable lodgings available practically next door to it, offered what Mabel felt to be an appropriate religious education for the boys and had far lower fees than King Edward's. Perhaps Ronald could flourish there? And so Mabel moved them to 26 Oliver Road, Edgbaston and placed both of the boys in St Philip's school. Of course, this caused more calamity in the family, but by this point Mabel was at least prepared for the backlash.

Alas, although Mabel was far happier in the heart of her chosen community, St Philip's was not what she had hoped for the boys. Hilary – now 8 – was doing well enough, but 10-year-old Ronald was still not achieving his potential. At first he flourished and soon he was top of the class, but without anything – or crucially any teachers – willing or able to intellectually challenge him, he floundered. Additionally, their standard of living was poor, Oliver Road had a bad reputation and Mabel, fed up with being let down by establishment after establishment, had had enough.

Supported by her friends in the Oratory, and her boys, she pulled Ronald and Hilary out of St Philip's, and home schooled them herself once more for several months, in preparation for the King Edward's entrance exams of 1903. And she was resoundingly successful. Not only did Ronald pass, but he was awarded a Foundation Scholarship. Although Hilary did not get in, Mabel quickly set the record straight, writing to a relative: 'not my fault… or that he didn't know the things but he is so dreamy and slow at writing'.[2] Mabel was happy to continue her tutelage of Hilary, and Hilary seemed content to learn at his own pace at home.

Ronald re-joined King Edward's in the sixth class (midway through the school) and quickly found his feet as before, this time finding a teacher and – of course – two languages that deeply inspired him.

The teacher was an assistant master named George Brewerton, Ronald's class teacher and a man with the unenviable position of teaching English literature (at that time a subject that barely featured on the curriculum and comprised almost entirely of Shakespeare) to schoolboys by rote learning, perhaps the worst possible way to introduce Shakespeare to anyone.

Ronald heartily loathed the Bard. However, that schoolboy's bitter frustration birthed one of Ronald's best ideas. In adulthood, writing to his close friend W.H. Auden, he recalled, '[the] bitter disappointment and disgust from schooldays with the shabby use made in Shakespeare of the coming of "Great Birnam Wood to high Dunsinane hill" [Malcolm's forces use tree limbs as camouflage, which Macbeth mistakes for the forest moving in his paranoia.] I longed to devise a setting by which the trees might really march to war.'[3] Of course, he did do just that, writing of the

Ents – sentient tree-like creatures who shepherded the Huorn – storming Isengard in *The Two Towers*.

But for now Mr Brewerton had to find another way to capture Tolkien's attention. He recognised that Ronald was sharp and enjoyed reading, so Brewerton reasoned that perhaps – if Shakespeare was not to Ronald's tastes – Chaucer might be, and he encouraged the whole class to read *The Canterbury Tales.* Ronald found these much more exciting, but there was something else that inspired him profoundly: that sometimes, as a treat, Brewerton would recite Chaucer's work in its original form, Middle English. Ronald was absolutely captivated. Like Welsh before it, hearing these words ignited within him a passion for linguistic discovery that would be lifelong.

Unfortunately, for all the good that Brewerton inspired in his student, it seems likely that Tolkien picked up one of his worse attitudes along the way. Brewerton had a stern temper and a profound hatred for words that were not 'plain English' (aka not Latinate or French in origin). This loathing was so profound that, if Brewerton heard one of his students use the word 'manure', he would scream at them to call it muck.[4]

Whilst in isolation this may seem like little more than an eccentricity, as with all academic beliefs and passions, it did not exist in a vacuum, and we can perhaps intuit that Brewerton held less-than-charitable views about the French from what his pupil grew up to believe. Tolkien shared Brewerton's passion for Middle English, and the linguistic and storytelling styles of that era, and disliked the 'romance' influences that came into the English canon post the Norman Conquest, not considering them truly English. This developed into the foetid bloom of lifelong bad feelings towards the French, ostensibly because emotionally, he felt the Norman Conquest of the eleventh century (and the changes to the English language that came with it) as if it was a recent tragic event.[5] However, of course that does not excuse his views, which remained in spite of serving alongside French soldiers in the First World War, being considered for the home front allied code-breaking effort of the Second World War, and the fact that it severely stilted his academic development. Tolkien became a linguist who could read and write French but barely speak it due to his own prejudices. It should be noted that Mabel did not share this prejudice. She spoke French herself, and affectionately compared Ronald to a 'Parisian modiste'[6] as a compliment for his knack at matching fabric shades. As unpleasant as it might be to shine a light on the more troubling aspects of Tolkien, it is necessary; a biography is not a portrait, it should not smooth away flaws, but rather note them to create as accurate and whole an image of the subject as possible.

In most instances, Tolkien's linguistic passions were more positively expressed. Aside from Middle English, the other language that he found inspiring at that time was Greek, describing his schoolboy fascination with it as, 'its surface glitter captivated me. But part of the attraction was antiquity and alien remoteness (from me): it did not touch home.'[7] It is interesting that there is a direct juxtaposition in how Tolkien responds to Greek and French: both are in some ways 'alien' to him, and both are now focused on at school.

Another of his linguistic passions was ignited outside of King Edward's, by Mabel's closest friend from the Oratory, Father Morgan. Father Francis Xavier Morgan was a jovial and kind man, and soon became a boisterous and outgoing addition to the quiet and reserved Tolkien household. He had studied under the Oratory's founder John Henry Newman. His maternal relatives were big names in the sherry business. And – most interesting for young Ronald's purposes – he was Anglo-Spanish on one side of his family, and Welsh on the other. He was loud, flamboyant even (which he attributed to his Spanish side). And he had just taken up the duties of parish priest when Mabel moved into the area.

From the moment he visited to introduce himself to the family, Mabel realised that she had found not only a good priest but a wonderful friend. He was sympathetic and an invaluable listening ear to her, and soon became seen as part of the family. At first, the children needed more convincing. Used to reading and playing quietly (at home at least, school for Ronald was a different matter) at first the boys found the 43-year-old Father Francis' exuberance startling, and his propensity to crack jokes embarrassing! But they soon came round to him, realising that he was a truly kind man who genuinely had their best interests at heart.

He tried to teach Ronald Spanish but ended up teaching him a little Welsh instead (though Ronald fondly identified him as Spanish throughout his life). He was a frequent visitor to the Tolkiens', and they frequented the Oratory regularly. Between him and May Incledon, Mabel finally had a grounding of good adult company to support her as she raised her boys. Life was of course still far from perfect, they were still always perilously close to the breadline, and Oliver Road was still difficult to live in, but she was no longer alone.

And so life continued in Edgbaston for the Tolkiens, almost entirely unlike Sarehole, but still leaving an influence on Ronald's young mind, though not necessarily a positive one. From Oliver Road, the early 1900's skyline was dominated by two towers: Perrott's Folly, a 29m tall isolated tower, and the Victorian tower of Edgbaston Waterworks, a lighthouse-like structure standing slightly behind the L-shaped main building from the road. These two towers, one (Perrott's Folly) a centuries-old anachronism standing alone, and the other intimately linked with modernity, industry and commodity, have been speculated to be the inspirations for the titular *Two Towers* of the second *Lord of the Rings* book. However, this is highly contested within Tolkien academia. For starters, it is unclear which of the many towers in *The Lord of the Rings* trilogy the title refers to in the books. The two largest camps are those who believe the title refers to Minas Tirith and Minas Morgul (fortified tower cities of the opposing sides of the book's conflict), and those who believe the *Two Towers* are Orthanc and Barad-dûr (Saruman and Sauron's respective bases of operations).

This book, much like Duriez and the writing team of the 2002 *Two Towers* film adaptation, favours the latter interpretation, as well as the possibility that the two towers of Edgbaston could have been the initial inspiration for them. Perrott's Folly – which is situated in the centre of Rotton Park and dwarfs all surrounding buildings – was being used as a weather recording station at the time, making it a strange isolated tower with odd equipment visible inside. This is something a young mind could easily find strange and eventually grow into Barad-dûr: an impossibly large dark fortress from whence the Eye of Sauron can be glimpsed from within the uppermost tower. Similarly, Edgbaston Waterworks' Victorian tower is very pretty in isolation, and being used to provide a vital function, yet it is being swallowed by the loud, industrial water processing plant, paralleling how Orthanc was once in harmony with nature, until Saruman switched his allegiance and turned it into the centrepiece of his industrial war machine. However, unlike many other tidbits of inspiration, Tolkien never publicly disclosed that Edgbaston's skyline influenced his work, so this is a purely speculative theory.

Back to 1903, and, in spite of everything, the Tolkien family was enjoying a blissful Christmas season. For starters, the boys found a misplaced postal order from their maternal grandmother for a small but helpful sum and used it to buy gifts for the family (Mabel contributing also, trusting the boys to buy the gifts from her as well), and both of them were keen artists, drawing a lot in their spare time.[8] Ronald had taken to drawing so much that several of his works were hanging in Father Francis' room as an 'exhibition' that winter.[9] Ronald was also flourishing at and outside of school, as he and his mother took self-improvement very seriously, giving themselves new projects over the winter after Ronald's school let out on 16 December. He was keeping up with his Greek, an Oratory priest was teaching him chess and encouraging his interests outside of reading. And finally, much to Mabel's joy, he took his first communion, on Christmas Day.

To see the knife-edge that Mabel had to walk in terms of navigating her extended family's reactions to what was for her nuclear family an important and happy occasion, here is an extract from a letter she wrote to her mother-in-law that winter:

'Ronald is making his First Communion this Christmas – so it is a very great feast indeed to us this year. I don't say this to vex you – only you say you like to know everything about them. Yours always lovingly, Mab.'[10]

Keeping the family informed of their business could mean welcome affection and even a small financial gift, but equally it could mean further anger and isolation, and often there was no telling which reaction she would receive. The stress of this isolation and abuse wore on her over the years, fraying her nerves as much as the poverty did. The family was perhaps one major catastrophe away from total implosion, and sadly that is exactly what 1904 brought.

The New Year, and Ronald's twelfth birthday two days after, were quickly overshadowed by a series of disasters. The cramped conditions of Ronald's school, the narrow soot-choked Oliver Road, the pollution of the city's industries, and the winter cold caused a health implosion in the household. The boys contracted measles, which then progressed into whooping cough for both of them. For Ronald, he managed to recover after whooping cough, but for Hilary it escalated into full-blown pneumonia. All three of these illnesses were potentially fatal for children at the time, and for Hilary to have one after the other was terrifying for his brother and mother. Especially for Mabel, who could remember Arthur – whose appearance and constitution was so similar to Hilary's – and how quickly he went from being hale and healthy to expiring miles from home. Mabel tried her best to nurse Hilary back to health, succeeding, but at a great cost. She lost weight and colour in her face. She was strained, and fraying in every aspect of her life. The Oratory helped her as best they could, but the mental and physical strain was too much.

After three long months of fighting her children's illnesses in the face of extreme poverty, she could take it no longer, and in April of 1904 Mabel Tolkien was hospitalised, and the small house on Oliver Road was no more. The few pieces of furniture she had were put into storage. The doors were closed, and her children taken to live with relatives: Hilary to Mabel's parents, and Ronald to her younger sister Jane and her husband (and the Suffields' former lodger), Edwin Neave. The children were presumably separated to reduce the risk of them re-infecting each other after recovering from such serious illnesses, but for two constant companions to be separated at such an already distressing time must have been frightening for them.

Mabel's parents, perhaps realising their folly in isolating their daughter only now, after seeing the toll it had taken on her health, welcomed Hilary into their home, where he continued to recover from his pneumonia and observe life in the city. Jane and Edwin Neave had Ronald to care for, and were glad to do so; after all, the Neaves' own marriage was something of an iconoclastic stir in the Suffield clan, so they knew a thing or two about being given the cold shoulder by the Birmingham side of the family. However, they had been able to move out of the city to the coast, in Hove, next door to Brighton.

By the sea, Ronald's health also improved, as it had all those years ago on that holiday to the Cape in South Africa. Time with the Neaves, as pleasant and welcoming as ever (though sadly we have no record of whether or not Edwin still played the banjo), must have felt like an oasis of calm in the midst of the turmoil Ronald was enduring, so far away from the city and the smog. Although the Sarehole-like Shire looms large in Tolkien's writings as a centre of homeliness, an undercurrent of coastal beauty runs through Middle-Earth. Specifically, Valinor (a form of paradise), can only be reached by the Elves and select outstanding individuals by 'sailing West' and undertaking a great metaphysical voyage. Elves, Tolkien's version of a romanticised Humankind who did not Fall, feel a specific longing to sail West after hearing the cry of a seagull, knowing then that their time on Middle-Earth is coming to its natural end and they must return to the sea and Valinor beyond it. That idea of the clarion call to ascend spiritually, and the deep significance of the sea and coast as a place of healing, is possibly traced back to Tolkien's time spent healing in Hove, where the coast sparkles beautifully at sunset and the cries of the gulls are plentiful.

Meanwhile, in Birmingham, Mabel's condition was improving and stabilising, but it came with worse news. She was diagnosed with diabetes. As it was not possible to manufacture insulin at the time, there was no way to safely and consistently manage the condition, so this diagnosis was considered fatal. Nonetheless, slowly but surely, Mabel got her strength back, and was able to be discharged in the summer of that year. However, the smog and stress of the city was disastrous to her health, as she and all of her close family and friends knew, so she needed a place for her and the boys to stay, away from Birmingham.

Here, Father Francis Morgan sprang into action. He had already gone above and beyond his priestly duties in providing some financial support for the Tolkiens, but now he worked hard to make arrangements for the Tolkiens to be united in a home they could truly recover in. The Oratory kept a small country retreat in the Worcestershire village of Rednal, which had been built in Cardinal Newman's time. In its grounds was a small cottage, where Mr and Mrs Till, the postman and his wife, lived. After hearing of the dire situation in Birmingham, the Tills volunteered a sitting-room and a bedroom for Mabel and the boys' use, and Mrs Till's cooking services.

The family gladly accepted, and so in June 1904, they moved to Rednal 'for the summer' (perhaps a white lie for the boys). Out there, in the countryside, still with the close ties to the Oratory community that Mabel valued so much, they were truly happy once again. There was a pleasant, easy routine for the boys, exploring the countryside or reading outside with Mabel, and regular visits and excursions with Father Francis. As Mabel wrote in a postcard to her mother-in-law:

'Boys look *ridiculously* well compared to the weak white ghosts that met me on the train 4 weeks ago!! ... We've had perfect weather. Boys will write first wet day but what with Bilberry-gathering –

Tea in Hay – Kite-flying with Father Francis – sketching – Tree-Climbing – they've never enjoyed a holiday so much.'[11]

Indeed there was something of an easy rhythm to their lives once more. The religious practices that had become so important to their mother were easy for her to observe, what with visiting clergy from the Oratory appearing often enough, but on the days when they weren't present Mabel, Ronald and Hilary would hitch a cart ride with the Churches – an elderly couple who were the Oratory House's housekeeper and gardener – to the nearest church. Mrs Till cooked them lovely meals, providing a great amount of respite for Mabel as she recovered, and Father Francis was a regular visitor. He had a dog, kept at the country house, called Lord Roberts, who the boys played with, and when he was not taking the boys on walks or flying kites with them he could often be found sitting on the Oratory House's veranda, surrounded by its creeping ivy, and smoking a large cherrywood pipe. This image stuck in Tolkien's mind as an adult, for Father Francis only ever smoked at the Oratory House, leading Ronald to 'blame' his own pipe addiction in later life on Father Francis' countryside smoking.

The summer was over all too soon and Ronald – fortunately healthy once more – had to return to school. However, Mabel was not leaving the countryside, and so the family stayed in Rednal. Although both the boys were much happier with this arrangement, this did leave Ronald with a commute into school that included a mile-long walk each way. He started his days early and came home late, so much so that by winter time Hilary often had to meet him at the station with a lantern. But still, life seemed to the children to be on the up; they lived in a beautiful, supportive place, had reconnected with some of their family prior to moving, and their mother's health seemed to be improving.

It is unknown if Mabel shielded the worst of her condition from her children, or if they were simply too young to comprehend what was happening to her, but her health was not improving. She deteriorated to more day-by-day, yet Ronald and Hilary did not notice, until one cold day in November she collapsed suddenly. Terrified, Ronald and Hilary sought help, and adults with stern faces gathered about the little cottage. Mabel would never recover. She had slipped into a diabetic coma, which she stayed in for six days. And, finally, on 14 November 1904, Mabel Tolkien died, at the age of 34, with only May Incledon and Father Francis at her bedside.

She was buried in St Peter's Roman Catholic Church, and, as a symbol of how devout and close she had been to the Oratory, her grave was marked with a cross strongly resembling the graves of the Oratory fathers.[12] In the spirit of their founder, Cardinal Newman, the Oratory celebrated Mabel as someone who genuinely gave her life to the church and her family. Francis and May recognised the depths of her strength of will and intelligence, and worked hard to honour her as best they could in the way she wished at her funeral.

The effect this had on Tolkien was of course devastating and profound. Both the trauma he felt and the faith he gained from Mabel's death were things he carried with him for the rest of his life. His faith was deeply tied to his feelings about Mabel, as he saw her almost as a form of martyr. In his own words as an adult:

'I witnessed (half-comprehending) the heroic sufferings and early death in extreme poverty of my mother who brought me into the Church; and received the astonishing charity of Francis Morgan. But I fell in love with the Blessed Sacrament from the beginning...'[13]

Additionally, the resentment he felt towards his mother's family for her isolation at their hands only deepened. Writing to his grandson in 1965, he still spoke of it with all the sound and fury of anger and grief still fresh.

'When I think of my mother's death (younger than Prisca [his only daughter Priscilla, then 36]) worn out with [family] persecution, poverty, and, largely consequent, disease, in the effort to hand on to us small boys the Faith, and remember the tiny bedroom she shared with us in rented rooms in a postman's cottage at Rednal, where she died alone, too ill for viaticum, I find it very hard when my children stray away.'[14]

Although both Ronald and Hilary remained in touch with most of their extended family throughout the rest of their lives, Ronald could never fully forgive them for what they did to Mabel.

But he remembered Mabel in other ways, as deeply gifted, but also profoundly interwoven and familiar with grief.[15] This connection Ronald made to her and grief, no doubt through witnessing her bear the loss of her husband and then her family ties, is an interesting one. Grief, and how it is processed, is an ongoing theme throughout all of the Middle-Earth writings. Of course, not all of it is tied to the loss of Mabel, Tolkien having lived through two world wars by the time *The Lord of the Rings* was published, but there are certain figures in his fantasy world that bear Mabel's shadow, the most prominent of whom is the Valar (angelic or god-like being) Nienna. One of the eight most powerful Valar in the legendarium, Nienna's element is grief. She wears a grey hood, and mourns for all of the evil in the world. The students of Nienna are blessed with her compassion and wisdom. (Gandalf is one of them, known for being a Maiar uncharacteristically interested in hearing out oft-neglected races or people, even feeling pity for the mistreatment of the Orcs by Saruman's hand.) Aside from Nienna's grieving association being so closely tied to teaching others and healing, which Tolkien also identified with his mother, in *The Silmarillion*, Nienna also causes nature to bloom and/or recover from the onslaught of dark forces with her tears, healing the plants bearing celestial light in the process. That Tolkien places such a profound significance on a wise female figure as the bastion and element of grief, after growing up watching his mother suffer greatly, cannot be overlooked. In fact, Tolkien seems to have taken a positive message from his experience: that grief can make you wiser and more empathetic.

And there was one more way in which Mabel left an impact on Tolkien. Throughout his life, he credited her with not only his early education, but also with igniting his passions for philology, language and fantastical stories.[16] As an adult, one who became a world-renowned philologist and fantasy storyteller, he attributed his start to Mabel. One hopes that he felt some peace in the knowledge that all he did in her memory would have made her so proud.

Chapter 4

The Lost and Found Boys

Orphaned at the ages of 10 and 12 respectively, their mother had been their whole world, and now she was gone. Grief and fear gripped the boys; they were not only without a mother, but also without any security. The life she had built for them depended on her being somewhat independent from the rest of their family due to their religion, and now once again that was threatened. But if one thing could be said of Mabel, it was that she had always (usually out of necessity) planned and plotted and fought tooth and nail for her boys to be provided for, and her dying days were no exception. But who could she trust? The majority of her family and her husband's, although courteous enough to her face, would struggle to honour her dying wish that the boys be raised Catholic. May would want to help, but Walter would put his foot down, as he had with May's own faith. And so she appointed the one person she could trust with the boys as their guardian: a friend who had become family – Father Francis Morgan.

But even then they were not safe. At the time of her death, Mabel Tolkien had scarce more than £800 in investments for the boys' futures. Fortunately, the Oratory allowed their priests to keep private capital, so Father Francis had his own funds from his family's sherry business, which he used to support the boys. Under his care they never wanted for essentials nor comforts. However, the Tolkiens and Suffields still posed a significant problem. They were still furious that the boys were being raised Catholic, and surely Father Francis' guardianship of the boys only added fuel to the fire. The Suffields and Tolkiens were scheming. Parties gossiped and talked behind closed doors. A vague plan emerged: to contest Mabel's will and whisk the boys off to a Protestant boarding school.[1] One can only imagine the trauma being ripped from the last familiar and supportive adults in their life would have had on them should their extended family have been successful, but, fortunately, Mabel had chosen their guardian wisely. The Spaniard was not to be so easily bested.

In short, Father Francis needed to find them a home with an understanding, or at the very least religiously disinterested party. He searched and searched and eventually found someone who seemed to be an ideal candidate. Beatrice Suffield was a recently widowed distant aunt. She had a spare room, no particular interest in religion and even lived close to the Oratory, which was to become the lynchpin of stability in the orphaned boys' lives. And so Ronald and Hilary went to live with their aunt.

However, all was not well in that house. Beatrice was suffering. She had lost her husband, lived in austere poverty, and had seemingly fallen into a deep depression from which she would not rise. She dressed in all black and kept her house quiet and still. As the days passed, her emotions dampened to the point where she barely remembered the appropriate way to respond to happiness, or sadness, or grief. And into that home, two sensitive boys reeling from the loss of their mother were encouragingly tipped over the threshold.

Hilary found some things to take joy in. He liked to throw small stones from his window to startle the cats milling below, but his brother took no joy in the view from their bedroom window. He missed his mother, and their life amidst nature. Here, in the city, he could see rolling hills in the distance, but industry spiked and loomed over it, dominating the landscape, and separating him from his heart-home. And something inside him broke. From this point forth he had seemingly two parts to himself: a boy (later a man) and his shadow. The shadow was not 'his true self' or anything quite so melodramatic, but instead merely an element within him he only let out to his closest companions and diaries. Other biographers have tried to capture it, and Carpenter put it best when he wrote,

'This side of him was capable of profound despair. More precisely, and more closely related to his mother's death, when he was in this mood he had a deep sense of impending loss. Nothing was safe. Nothing would last. No battle would be won for ever.'[2]

It is entirely possible that this was chronic depression, or even situation depression; after all, Tolkien endured two world wars and a shocking amount of childhood grief and trauma. Additionally, Beatrice Suffield seems – from what records we have of her – to have been deeply depressed during Hilary and Ronald's time under her roof, and a traumatised child in that situation might also absorb the behaviour of an adult charged in part with their care. With her the Tolkien boys' home was quiet and still and grey. Hilary missed playing outside. Ronald missed the countryside. And both boys were profoundly unhappy. In adult life, Ronald even wrote of what must have been a heartbreaking moment for him. Returning home one day, he found that Beatrice had recently lit a fire. In the ashy remains, he found all of his mother's letters and personal papers. She had not even considered that these might be of emotional importance to the boys, and did not understand the hurt they felt at her actions.

Beatrice was unfit, and perhaps unable, to care for these children, but outwardly all appearances seemed fine. Upon Father Francis' visits it was clear they were fed and watered. Their room was not damp or mouldy, but inside the boys were starved of positive adult caregivers. Father Francis was there for them as much as he was able to be, but he still had his duties to the Oratory, and regular visits and outings were no replacement for a parent. We may never know for certain why the Tolkien boys did not tell him that they were unhappy in their lodgings, but it seems as if they felt a sense of ungratefulness. Father Francis – so jolly and kind – was helping them more than anyone else, and they could not bring themselves to 'let him down' by telling him that the home he had worked so hard to find them was not a home anymore.

Of course, it was not all doom and gloom. In fact, what would become one of Ronald's most famous and enduring passions blossomed at this time in his life, and it began with another of the few remaining ties to his past life: the Incledons. May invited her late sister's children into her house often (this was where the boys spent their holidays after their mother's passing), for they were close to her own children, two girls of similar ages: Marjorie and her younger sister Mary. Furthermore, the two girls were just as creatively minded as their Tolkien cousins. Their fondness was for animals, whilst the boys preferred plants, but they played together often and the four cousins remained close throughout their childhood. But there was one game that Ronald saw them play that fascinated him, and ignited something in his own mind. Marjorie and Mary sometimes spoke to each other in a language of their own invention. Both of them were still quite young, so it was a simple language, largely comprised of loan words from English repurposed to suit their own needs. As it was principally comprised of animal names, they called it Animalic.

The already linguistically fascinated Ronald was eager to join in on this game, and his cousins welcomed him, bringing the worldwide total of Animalic-speakers to a sound three. Animalic was a simple language, and seems to have primarily been used to communicate rude phrases or nonsense between its speakers without detection by adults (one of the few surviving phrases we have is 'Dog nightingale woodpecker forty', which roughly translates to 'you are an ass', for example!).

Perhaps it was outgrowing her sister and cousin's humour that caused Marjorie to lose interest in Animalic, and in creating languages altogether after a while, or perhaps, a desire to feel grown-up by affecting being above it all. Whatever the reason, Marjorie made it clear to Mary and Ronald that she did not wish to create languages anymore. Not that this deterred the two of them. In fact, Mary and Ronald's first language-creating collaboration was far more complex than Animalic. Called *Nevbosh* 'or the New Nonsense' (Mary and Ronald liked to play at giving their language a sense of dictionary-like pedigree and history), Nevbosh had neologisms, its own grammar, and sentence structure, to the point where rhyming limericks could be created.[3]

Now that the language-making bug had bitten him, Ronald found it deeply infectious. Not content just to play at it with Mary, he began to create them in his own time as a solo hobby. Already proficient in Greek and Latin (though still as yet unable to fully connection with Welsh yet due to a paucity of age-appropriate resources), he was desperate to add another tongue to his quiver. Father Francis was fluent in Spanish, and his charge begged him to teach him, but for whatever reason he never got around to it. Instead, he lent Ronald all of his Spanish books, and that satiated the young boy for now, as well as forming the basis of his own invented language. *Naffarin*, as Ronald called it, borrowed heavily from Spanish and lightly from Ronald's other spoken languages, but it was a little more complex than Nevbosh, which built on the building bricks of Mary and Marjorie's Animalic before it. Each iteration of the creative process improved upon the last, like a novice musician learning more and more complex pieces, improving their form as they learn. In fact, as Carpenter put it, 'if he had been interested in music he would very likely have wanted to compose melodies, so why should he not make up a personal system of words that would be as it were a private symphony?'[4]

Aside from their holidays with their cousins, the boys had one other place where they felt calm, safe and happy: the Oratory. Although they could not live there, the Oratory did provide the boys with as much as they were able. Each morning before school the boys would serve Mass for Father Francis (ideally at his favourite side-altar), eat breakfast in the refectory, and then spin the (extremely patient and sweet-natured) kitchen cat around on the revolving food-hatch, before walking to school together. In another stroke of good fortune (though in no small part due to his work through an extremely difficult period of his life), Hilary had by now passed the King Edward's entrance exam. If the boys were on time, they would walk the whole way to school, but if they were running late (spinning that cat was extremely entertaining) there was a horse-bus they could hop onto to make it on time.

Seeing how not just Father Francis, but the Oratory as a whole reached out to and protected the two boys, it is clear why faith became such a crucial part of Tolkien's life. The Oratory offered a very literal sanctuary after Mabel's passing, and as Tolkien's own faith was so rooted in his mother's it also helped him grieve and heal as best he could from her passing. Perhaps this is why Healing Houses play such a large part in Tolkien's work. Nienna's abode where she comforts the deceased is a healing house as such, and the ultimate comfort in the afterlife; a space where the dead can take all the time in the world to grieve every single loss they felt in life. However, perhaps the most prominent Houses of Healing are those where Faramir, Merry and Éowyn recovered after the Battle of Pelinor Fields. This building (and its inhabitants) crucially heals not only physical wounds but the deep spiritual scarring of having faced Sauron's forces. Interestingly, Tolkien's views on his own grief might be represented in what Merry and Éowyn experience. After the duo slay the Witch King of Angmar, Black Breath from his body enters theirs, causing a soul crushing despair. Their time in the Houses of Healing does heal and recuperate them, but every year for the rest of their lives the blackness would return and they would feel the pang of their wounds once more. Here we see a restorative but impermanent kind of peace offered by a place and building of solace, perhaps reflective of how Tolkien processed his own grief. Faith, people and places can offer comfort, heal wounds, but the injury never leaves.

If home was the Oratory and holidays at the Incledons, both Ronald and Hilary needed further support to endure life in Beatrice's care. Fortunately, both Hilary and Ronald found that at school, and in the case of some of Ronald's friends, these connections were lifelong.

The first close school chum Ronald had was one such person. Christopher Wiseman was his name. Christopher and Ronald saw themselves as complementary opposites in many ways. Where Ronald was a linguist with a Grecian and Gothic bent, Wiseman was drawn to the hieroglyphs of Middle Egyptian. Christopher was a Methodist to Ronald's Catholic. Where Ronald followed the humanities and literature, Christopher was more drawn to the sciences. And where Ronald created languages for fun, Christopher's passion was music. They both loved Arthurian legends and archaeology, and were avid rugby players, to the point where they held the nickname (for themselves) of 'The Great Twin Brethren'.[5] They were so alike academically that they often placed first and second in tests, and so were in the same class from 1905 onwards. Aside from their academic and sporting activities, they enjoyed discussing their faith with each other from a young age, as well as philosophising and debating their thoughts and feelings.

Perhaps these practice bouts with Christopher spurred Ronald into another one of his treasured schoolboy pastimes: debating. Ronald was an avid debater, choosing to debut with a controversial topic for the time, 'That this house expresses its sympathy with the objects and its admiration for the tactics of the Militant Suffragette.'[6] On that occasion he spoke well, but throughout his academic career he varied from being a confident and commanding orator to being infamous for wandering off-topic and slurring his speech so much he could barely be understood. Additionally, as he gained confidence in the debating society, he started to use the space to pontificate on some of his more esoteric passions. Once he spoke on the 'bastardisation' of the English language by the Norman Conquest. On another occasion, he broke off from the main point he was making to go on an extended rant about Shakespeare's shortcomings in his eyes as a writer and entertainer. Student and teachers alike seemed to view Ronald with curiosity and confusion; on the one hand he was clearly a very intelligent boy, with a genuine passion for academia and an unquenchable thirst for knowledge, on the other he was a lazy student who could not focus and did not apply himself.

In later life, his friend C.S. Lewis recalled how Tolkien would describe himself as an idle student, the bane of his headmaster, when in reality he was beavering away studying Welsh, Old English and Gothic in his spare time, on top of his schoolwork and forging his own languages.[7] Ronald was a more than capable scholar, but his wants and needs were not being satisfied by the curriculum (nor, often, the teaching methods) of the time. Ronald needed something substantial to fuel his first academically rigorous forays into linguistics. Fortunately, not only was the school's headmaster, Gilson, classically educated (as was customary for the time) and therefore familiar with Latin and Greek, he was also a proactive educator, eager to pass on his passion to his students. So much so that he ran extra lessons on New Testament Greek, which Ronald diligently attended.

It was perhaps through here that he met another of his dear friends, Gilson's son, Robert Quilter Gilson. Also a student at his father's school, Robert's passion and skills lay in painting and drama, and he bonded with Ronald – who was still an avid sketch artist – over art. However, there was a deeper, more emotional bond the boys shared. Robert's mother had also died whilst Robert was still a child, and his father had remarried in 1907. Both boys helped each other through their parental loss, and developed an honest and complex friendship through it.

These three boys were all passionate scholars, but also all a bit mischievous and easily bored by the constraints of regurgitative rote-learning education and strict school rules of the time. Ronald's mind wandered. Robert's creativity did not fit into his father's rigidly academic school, nor did Christopher's preference for hieroglyphs and music over dusty school tomes. And so the three would often meet to study together in the library, sharing their burden and chattering amongst themselves. However, they felt that they were very much missing something to make the whole experience of studying go down quicker: afternoon teas. There was one problem with this desire: the school did not permit eating in the library. And so the boys started a conspiracy, uniting to sneak tea, cakes and various other snacks into the library and consume them without being caught.

In later life, Christopher Wiseman recounted how they had done it. They hid food in their satchels, smuggled a full tea set in (which they then hid in the shelves) and somehow boiled tea and set out full plates at the back of the library without detection! The finishing touch of their scheme was to stay in the library for as long as possible, until the cleaners came by with large buckets, and then surreptitiously dump the remaining tea water in there and sneak out. And for the most part they were successful, though there were certainly times when it all went awry. Wiseman recalled a time when someone brought in tinned fish, which was an unpopular and therefore unfinished snack. Nobody wanting to take home the pungent stuff, they stashed it on a shelf, out of sight and out of mind until it was detected by smell by the staff.[8]

Another of the boys' favourite haunts were the tea shops in town, their favourite being the Barrow Stores teashop, which opened in 1905 when the boys were 16. Over time, this led to the boys referring to themselves as the Tea Club and Barrovian Society, or TCBS, as they formally declared themselves in 1911.

With their penchant for creative rule-breaking and fun pastimes, the TCBS soon gained a reputation, and with it popularity, among the schoolboys. Their numbers swelled, but these new TCBS boys were seen by the core three as lacking in the serious desire to be the artistic brethren that the trio saw themselves as, and were instead more interested in eating treats in the library.

There was also a third boy from this era of Tolkien's life who made a lasting impression on him, and who perhaps would have been a part of the creative brethren that made up the core TCBS, had his health not failed. Vincent Trough was his name. Although a little younger than Ronald, his interests aligned with the other boys well. He was fond of sports, took great delight in making puns, and was an avid debater, though he was often slow to make his point, speaking in what was referred to as a 'dreamy, weary fashion'.[9] But beyond these surface-level schoolboy interests, Vincent had something which tied him to the creative spirits at the heart of the TCBS: he was an amateur poet. However, another thing Vincent had in common with Tolkien was ill health, and in the autumn of 1911 (after Tolkien had graduated from King Edward's and was in his first year at university) he was invalided out of school entirely to convalesce in Cornwall. Unfortunately, he never recovered. Vincent Trough died in January of 1912. His TCBS friends grieved him, but Tolkien – late to receive the news of his passing and unable to get from his college rooms to Cornwall so suddenly – was unable to attend his friend's funeral, only able to contribute towards a wreath from the TCBS as a means to pay his respects. Trough has the macabre distinction of being the first of Tolkien's childhood friends to die suddenly, but unfortunately he would not be the last.

As strange and perhaps pretentious as that sounds, as the surviving TCBS boys grew up the TCBS *did* grow with them, into a brethren of creatives with a studious and philosophical bent, who enjoyed sharing their work and projects with each other and philosophising together. But before they fully bloomed into what they desired to be, they did gain a new 'real' member, a replacement for their dear friend Vincent, after Tolkien himself had moved out of Birmingham altogether.

Being the headmaster's son, Gilson was the most proactive and connected to the school amongst the boys, and so it was through him that this new member was found. Gilson's passion for drama often led to him directing and/or starring in school plays, and this was the case with his final year piece: a production of R.B. Sheridan's *The Rivals*. Naturally, the other members of the TCBS could be found on the cast list (and Gilson coincidentally played the hero; one imagines that being the headmaster's son allowed him a degree of privilege in his casting and directing choices not typically allowed to school students…). However, there was another member of the cast, three years their junior, who Gilson noticed and introduced into the TCBS fold. Geoffrey Bache Smith (G.B. Smith as he came to be known) was a sensitive young man, with an interest in modern literature and – in an echo of Vincent Trough – dreams of becoming a poet.

Tolkien had to travel back to his school to perform in the play (in which he played Mrs Malaprop, a comedic character who, as her name suggests, frequently gets words and sayings completely wrong, a fun part for the linguist, no doubt). And by all surviving accounts, it seemed to be worth it, for *The Rivals* was a hit. In fact, a report from the school newspaper (*The King Edward's School Chronicle*) actually gives mention to all four TCBS members and their performances:

'J.R.R. Tolkien's Mrs Malaprop was a real creation, excellent in every way and not least so in make-up. Rob Gilson as Captain Absolute made a most attractive hero, bearing the burden of what is a very heavy part with admirable spirit and skill; and as the choleric old Sir Antony, CL Wiseman was extremely effective. Among the minor characters, G.B. Smith's rendering of the difficult and thankless part of Faulkland was worthy of high praise.'[10]

From these friendships, formed during or just after these schooldays, we see that Tolkien found comfort in small, close friendship groups, where he shared a unique emotional bond with each of the members. Wiseman was his complementary colour on the wheel: opposite but in a way that emboldened Ronald to achieve his best. Gilson was a fellow creative mind who sought comfort in his works after the trauma of losing his mother. And G.B. Smith was something of a kindred spirit. He had an untameable honest creative voice, which he mainly expressed through his poetry. And he was so passionate about modern literature that even a stalwart (and somewhat narrow-minded on this matter) traditionalist like Ronald had to acquiesce and agree that there was profound beauty and worth in modern poetry and prose. Similarly, GB adored Ronald's work, vociferous in his praise both in writing and person.

The two pushed each other creatively as only truly equal relationships can, but even before GB came into his life Ronald could always rely on his dear friends in the TCBS for support and inspiration.

It is easy to look at this group of four friends Tolkien had from childhood to young adulthood and make a one-to-one comparison with the four hobbits in the Fellowship of the Ring. However, I would argue that that perhaps flattens Tolkien's work to direct allegory, which it never was. None of the hobbits 'are' Christopher or Rob or Geoffrey, but rather those formative friendships are reflected in the nature of male friendship in both *The Hobbit* and *The Lord of the Rings*. Fittingly, as the story is for much younger children, in *The Hobbit* we see close friendships as they may appear to a child who has yet to fully conceptualise the world outside themself. Bilbo's friendships with the Dwarves of Erebor are close but (on Bilbo's side, at any rate) transactional; he is fond of the Dwarves so long as his bond with them never pushes him too far out of his comfort zone, and never demands too much of him. He does not understand their quest to reclaim the halls and treasures of their ancestors, to him it is a 'holiday', a chance to see the world beyond the Shire. When confronted with demands from the Dwarves to do the job they hired him for, he lashes out; preserving his xenophobic tantrum in-universe for all of the Shire to see in his internal monologue about what he sees as cowardice of his loyal and kind travelling companions of six months. In the crucial battle for Erebor, Bilbo goes so far as to switch allegiances to the Elves (who had previously imprisoned and psychologically tormented the Dwarves) because he is awed by their aesthetics and 'noble nature'. By the end of the book, Bilbo does mature: apologising to Thorin Oakenshield, but only on the latter's deathbed. The book almost reads as a coming of age story for a man well into his adulthood, allowed a perpetual dawn of immaturity by his wealth, status, lack of awareness and absence of responsibility. This is not to accuse Tolkien of immaturity or childishness or a lack of empathy – far from it – but simply to raise the point that he writes a childlike protagonist very well.

By the time of *The Lord of the Rings*, Bilbo is more mature and no longer the protagonist, and instead the friendship dynamics focused are those of Frodo, his gardener Sam, and his cousins Merry and Pippin. Here you see the complex friendships formed and explored. Interestingly, when the hobbits first set out on their journey, Frodo – much like his uncle before him – tries to treat his relationship with Sam as transactional, trying to get Sam to draw baths for Frodo and the other hobbits (all upper-class hobbits, unlike Sam, a working-class labourer), and has to be reminded by Pippin (ironically the highest status hobbit of the four) that now that they are on this quest together, there should be no distinction between the others and Sam. In turn, Frodo apologises and makes an effort to change his ways, and the deep and enduring friendship that develops between Frodo and Sam becomes one of the emotional lynchpins of the whole epic. Conversely, Sam also flourishes under the encouragement of people who now see him as friends and not staff; he recites his poetry to the group, offers his own opinions, and learns to value his own voice.

It is in these subtle dynamic shifts; these hobbit friendships of checks and balances, where love for another person is not mindless loyalty but the courage to speak up when they do something wrong, that we can perhaps see the influence of the friendships with the TCBS. In particular how these moments of temporary friction tend to lead to moments of creative or personal actualisation: Sam's poetry and courage, Pippin's responsibility, Merry's defiance of an unjust system, and Frodo's empathy.

All of these are traits the hobbits forge for themselves, but are ignited by these sparks between friends.

Back in twentieth-century Birmingham, the Tolkien boys cobbled together a home out of everywhere they did not live: the Oratory, the Incledons' home, their school-time haunts, but there was one other place, and time, when they could have something resembling a family. Every year, without fail, Father Francis Morgan (again, off his own bat, and not Mabel's instructions) would take the boys on a summer holiday with him. They would go to the West Dorset coastal town of Lyme Regis, a spot known for cliffside walks, ample rocky seaside and fossil-hunting. Every year they stayed in a hotel called the Three Cups, and every year they would divide their time between visiting Father Francis' friends in the town, and walking the cliffs and seaside. A fan of the outdoors and the coast, Ronald of course treasured these vacations. His favourite activity was to meander along the seashore looking at the flora and fauna, but even if it rained he was content to sketch the scenery from his window. But the real excitement of the trip was fossil-hunting at the mudslip in the cliff face. Part of the Jurassic Coast, this site is a bounty for amateur fossil-hunters even to this day, as well as a place of beauty in its own right: the seam from with the fossils flow is a rich blue-grey clay which pours out gently like a fantastical river. It is small wonder then that young Ronald, upon finding a fossilised jaw, immediately decided it was that of a 'petrified dragon',[11] for the cliff lent itself more to fantasy than reality at the best of times.

But the trip was more than an opportunity to treat the boys to some wonderment at nature, it was also Father Francis' time to reconnect with the boys, away from the religious formality of the Oratory and the smoke of the city. He spoke with them as much as he could, and eventually, one holiday, they finally let slip that they were not happy living with Beatrice. Contrary to what they had expected, Father Francis was not upset, nor did he think them ungrateful, but rather he was sad they had not told him sooner. When they returned, he immediately set about trying to find them a better place to live. Soon he fell upon a grand idea: there was a lady by the name of Mrs Faulkner, who lived close to the Oratory. She seemed a friendly and jolly sort; she had a love of music, and often invited the priests to musical soirées at her house. Furthermore, she rented rooms, and even had a young lodger close to Ronald's age at the time. Everything seemed a perfect fit. The house would not be gloomy and hostile to young boys, far from it; in fact, it was crowded with people, much like the Suffield house. There was Mrs Faulkner herself, her wine merchant husband (who was somewhat over fond of his own product), Helen, their daughter, Annie their maid and this lodger, a young lady with a talent for music.

And so, in 1908, Ronald and Hilary found themselves on the doorstep of the ivy-choked number 37 of Duchess Road. They were to spend most of the rest of their childhoods there, surrounded by people who were either indifferent to them or treated them harshly, with one exception: the raven-haired, grey-eyed 19-year-old in the first floor room: a young lady by the name of Edith Bratt.

Chapter 5

Mabel, Belladonna, Edith, Lúthien

E dith Bratt was born out of wedlock to Frances Bratt on 21 January 1889 in Gloucester. The Bratt family had some renown in Wolverhampton as footwear manufacturers, so it seems that the pregnant 30-year-old Frances was swept to Gloucester to save face. Whether or not Edith knew who her father was has been lost to time, for if she had the information she did not pass it on to another living soul. But her early years – much like those of Ronald and Hilary – were largely content if unorthodox. She was raised by her mother Frances and her older cousin Jennie Grove in Handsworth. Much like the Tolkiens, the Groves (and the Bratt family connected to the Groves by marriage) were extremely proud of their family connection to renown through music, for their relative, Sir George Grove, was somewhat famous for being the editor of the musical dictionary.

Edith herself turned out to also be a talented and creative musician. Her instrument of choice was the piano, so when her mother died (when Edith was just 14) her legal guardian, the family solicitor, sent her to a boarding school for girls which specialised in music. Girls who graduated were expected to become piano teachers or even concert pianists, and Edith was certainly talented enough to have been able to pursue the latter path. However, here Edith's luck ran out. Her guardian wasn't sure what to do with her next. Edith had inherited a small amount of land around Birmingham, and that was enough to sustain her financially, so perhaps (in the solicitor's mind) there was no urgent need to assist her in her career. So he found her the room at Mrs Faulkner's (presuming that Mrs Faulkner's love for music would be helpful to Edith) and left it at that.

And so it was that by the time the Tolkien boys moved into Mrs Faulkner's second floor bedroom, orphaned pianist and landowner Edith Bratt, now a slim, ethereal-featured 19-year-old, was still lodging in the first floor room. Unfortunately, her guardian's gamble on the Faulkner home being a nurturing environment for Edith's musical talents had not paid off. Mrs Faulkner greatly enjoyed the prestige of having a lodger who could play for her at soirées, but she hated to hear her practice, shooing her away from the upright if she tried to. And so Edith mostly hid herself in her bedroom, working on her sewing machine. Where Ronald's creative outlets were language and drawing, hers were music and sewing. But unlike Ronald, she was almost completely alone. She had no siblings, no school friends who visited, no Father Francis who wanted the best for her. The family solicitor seemed ambivalent to her fate at best, happy to let her languish in a house where she could not practice her craft as he was. And unlike Mabel, Frances was unable to provide Edith with more than a limited education. An illegitimate girl child of a well-to-do family who barely saw to her upkeep, her options were either to teach or play piano or marry into wealth.

And so the grey-eyed teenager who greeted Ronald and Hilary at Mrs Faulkner's had something of a conflicting air to her. She was playful and bold, begging Mrs Faulkner's maid Annie for foodstuffs which she would then hide in her room, to later invite the (often hungry) Tolkien boys for 'secret feasts', but there was more than a tinge of fatality and sadness to her. She was stuck in purgatory, waiting for someone to put her needs first, lest she while away her days a spinster with no profession and scarcely any money to her name.

There seem to be echoes of young Edith in Tolkien's most famous work. The character of Éowyn in *The Lord of the Rings* is similarly spirited but melancholic. As her uncle (King Théoden) succumbs to dark magics controlling his will, she is powerless to stop the death of her cousin and the banishment of her brother. This is not due to lacking spirit; she is proficient in swordsmanship and eager to help protect her uncle's kingdom, but due to being female she is excluded from the very hierarchy she is trying to fight for, pushed into diplomatic duties when she wishes to (and is more than capable of) riding into battle. When the reader is introduced to Éowyn, she is identified by her deep despair, and Gandalf the White has to admonish her brother for not doing his bit to support her. Infamously, the restored King Théoden forbids her to fight, in spite of her training, due to her gender. However, this spurs her into action: by teaming up with a fellow unlikely hero, Merry Brandybuck the Hobbit, they fight at the Battle of Pelinor Fields and slay the Witch King of Angmar.

It is not just in Éowyn as a character that parallels can be drawn between Edith and Ronald, but in her friendship with Merry. For entirely different reasons, both hobbit and maiden are ignored and/or dissuaded to fight by the men of Rohan, but together they unite and slay the Witch King of Angmar, whose black magic can be seen as analogous to depression. Tolkien identified himself with hobbits, and perhaps a shadow of the joy of the friendship he formed with an ethereal maiden overlooked by her family and the world is reflected in Merry and Éowyn.

For Ronald and Edith did fast become firm friends. Although three years apart in age (him being 16 and her being 19 when they met) they quickly became each other's closest confidants. They were united against 'the Old Lady' (Mrs Faulkner). They shared the food Annie gave Edith. They started to go to teashops in Birmingham together. Their favourite had a balcony that overhung the street below. Being together kindled a mischief in both of them, and they used to sit at a first-floor window seat and throw sugar lumps into the hats of passers-by, moving from table to table as each sugar bowl ran empty.

As their friendship deepened, so too did their extravagant gestures and clandestine methods of greeting each other to talk, to the point where they developed a secret whistle. In early morning or late evening, Edith would whistle at her window and Ronald would rush to his to see her staring up at him, so they could talk awhile undiscovered. For two such creative and mature teens, talking was their main attraction to each other. Anywhere they could talk, they would. At the Old Lady's fireside. At the teashops. At their windows before they were meant to be up, or after they were supposed to be in bed.

Unsurprisingly, these two teenagers, starved of affection and attention from others, eventually began a chaste romance. It was the summer of 1909 when they 'decided' they were in love.[1] According to Ronald, years later, their first kiss was 'almost accidental!'[2] However, both of them didn't seem to much mind the accident, and continued to visit teashops together, and meet to talk, only now as secret loves. It does indeed seem to be a puppy love they shared, not only because both parties were deeply religious (Catholic and Anglican respectively) but also because they were both romantics. Love was to them, wide-eyed, avid poetry-readers that they were, more of an emotional than physical experience. They wrote many a love letter to each other, and the most scandalous they ever got was to describe kisses, and even then in virtually no detail. They enjoyed picnicking and letter-writing and talking, seemingly focused on filling that gap in affection they both had since youth.

Interestingly, the clandestine nature of their relationship mirrors Arthur Tolkien and Mabel Suffield's romance, all those years before. Arthur proposed to Mabel shortly after she turned 18, and the Suffields forbade their union for at least two years due to him being thirteen years her senior. In this time, they could not see each other (unless at a family gathering where the Suffields were present to chaperone). Instead, they passed love letters to each other via a proxy, Jane, Mabel's younger sister.[3] Come rain or shine, Jane would wait at Birmingham New Street station platform to both deliver and receive letters from Arthur. And eventually, five years later, the two were wed in unusual circumstances.

It is quite bizarre how Edith and Ronald ended up paralleling Ronald's parents in so many ways. Although they were not kept apart by family, their guardians and landlady would have certainly considered it scandalous for the two of them to have a relationship, in part due to their difference in age (though Edith's three years of seniority was nowhere near as scandalous as Arthur's thirteen).

But unfortunately, as with many a secret love affair before it, it could not remain a secret forever. Near the end of Ronald's autumn term, he and Edith decided to spend a day together in the Lickey Hills. They planned their meeting down to the last detail, or so they thought. Edith rode off on her bike 'to visit her cousin Jennie Grove' (the woman who had helped raise her). Ronald rode off at a separate time 'to go to his school's sports ground'. They took different roads, and met up in the Lickey Hills to spend the afternoon together, and went home at different times. The perfect crime.

Except for one thing. Their fondness for taking tea together proved to be their undoing. They went into a Rednal village in search of a good place to take tea, and ended up choosing a house Ronald had often studied in. The lady who served them teas knew Ronald from his time studying there. And she told Mrs Church, the Oratory House caretaker whom the Tolkiens had known since Mabel's last days, that Ronald was with an unknown girl. And this started a chain of gossip that eventually led its way to Father Francis Morgan.

One can only imagine the sense of betrayal Father Francis felt when word got to back to him that Ronald, for whom he was sacrificing his money and time to raise, all in the hopes that the bright boy would have all the opportunities and support to makes something of himself, only to find out that he was instead entertaining the lodger three years his senior. Not only was their age difference a shock, but also the timing of their relationship. The reason why Ronald had been studying at a house separate to Mrs Faulkner's was that he was trying out for the Oxford scholarship. Father Francis firmly believed that Ronald was gifted and would flourish in an academic environment, just as Mabel had hoped for him. And now (coincidentally just around the time he started romancing Miss Bratt), at this crucial moment when he needed to be utmost focused on his studies, his mind was elsewhere. This was devastating for the priest, for Ronald had to not only gain a place at such a prestigious institution, but also to gain marks high enough for a scholarship, because Father Francis could not support him at Oxford from his own pocket.

Now, Ronald was by nature very intelligent, but his mind was prone to wander, and he struggled to focus on a single topic of study. The slipping marks could have been any number of Ronald's other interests: anything from the Debating Society, to rugby, to inventing his languages, or a combination of these things, but Father Francis had always known Ronald to be distracted by these frivolities. Edith was new.

And so he called him into the Oratory. What followed was a stern dressing down of Ronald and an establishment of a set of rules that broke Ronald's heart. Ronald was now to focus solely on his studies. And his relationship with Edith must cease immediately. Father Francis made arrangements for him and Hilary to be lodged elsewhere, and that was the end of that.

Ronald, still very much in love, though heartbroken, complied. He felt a tremendous affection to Father Francis, as well as guilt for having let his kindly guardian down. And in the midst of this maelstrom of emotions and losses, both of Edith and the respect of his father figure, he had to sit the Oxford entrance exam.

Unsurprisingly, he did not pass. However, travelling to Oxford and sitting the exam did do him some good. Staying in Corpus Christi College, seeing the beautiful architecture, the famed 'dreaming spires', he realised how much he would like to go there. This was momentous for him; he had had little gauge for what university life would be like, but now that he had tasted it he realised how much he wanted it for himself.

Fortunately, he would have another opportunity to prove himself. He could retake the exam the following December, but that really would be his last chance.

Throughout his life, Tolkien kept diaries only to process and vent his darker feelings, and it is perhaps telling that the first surviving diary we have from him is at this time, when Father Francis is disappointed in him, Edith is separated from him, and he has let himself down. On New Year's Day of 1910 he wrote, 'Depressed and as much in the dark as ever. God help me.'[4]

As for Edith, her position was equally humiliating and precarious. Mrs Faulkner was more overtly hostile towards her, as she was now the subject of a minor scandal. Her closest friend was taken from her, leaving her alone again. Interestingly, Jennie Grove, her stalwart cousin, seems to have stood by her during this difficult time, for the two remained close for Jennie's whole life. But Birmingham was no longer a welcoming home for Edith. She needed to get away.

Fortunately, an elderly solicitor and wife had befriended her, and were sympathetic to her situation, or at the very least willing to turn a blind eye. They invited her to live in their home in Cheltenham, and she accepted. Knowing her time in Birmingham, and perhaps in Ronald's life, was short, they had to make the most of the time they had left. Upon discovering that she was to move out of Birmingham altogether, he wrote two words in his diary: 'Thank God'.[5] This removed temptation and chance encounters from the equation. Perhaps he could truly settle down and focus as his guardian wanted him to.

Although Ronald could not bring himself to directly disobey his guardian, he was not above looking for technicalities to dodge around to allow he and Edith to see each other again. Father Francis had forced them to break up and live apart, but he had not said anything about never *seeing* each other again... and so the pair hatched one last plan, in the winter snow of January 1910. They were both January babies, so decided to meet in secret, two days in a row, to celebrate each other's birthdays. On the first day they went into town together, walking and talking as they had so many times before, but with the sense of melancholy and grandiose that they were both accustomed to this time feeling more earned. They went into a jeweller's shop. Edith bought Ronald a fine fountain pen, to celebrate his eighteenth birthday. Ronald bought her a wristwatch for her twenty-first. It cost 10 shillings and 6d. Perhaps they found some poetic symmetry in their gifts: the pianist gifting the writer a pen, and the writer gifting the pianist a way to keep time.

The next day, for Edith's birthday, they took tea together one last time. Although seated in a window seat as was their wont, now did not seem to be the time for throwing sugar lumps, so the hats below them went unseasoned.

If only they had had the forethought to sit away from the window, for, unfortunately, they were seen once again. And this time, when word got round to Father Francis, he was no longer disappointed. He was angry. Ronald was summoned to the Oratory once more, and this time Father Francis was deadly clear in his wording. Ronald was not to see Edith again, save for to see her off on her train to Cheltenham. But after that Ronald could not visit, communicate or even write to Edith for the entirety of the time Father Francis was his legal guardian, which would cease when Ronald turned 21. In short, Ronald was to be separated from his beloved for three years, which seems a terribly long time for any 18-year-old. Ronald was miserable.

But as luck would have it, chance encounters were still possible, even with Ronald fully obeying the letter and spirit of Father Francis' law. His diary from the time reads:

[16 February] 'Last night prayed would see E. by accident. Prayer answered. Saw her at 12.55 at Prince of Wales. Told her I could not write and arranged to see her off on Thursday fortnight. Happier but so much long to see her just once to cheer her up. Cannot think of anything else.'

[21 February] 'I saw a dejected little figure sloshing along in a mac and tweed hat and could not resist crossing and saying a word of love and cheerfulness. This cheered me up a little while.'

And finally [23 February] 'I met her coming from the cathedral to pray for me.'[6]

Clearly both were deeply despondent without each other. Edith's moods and emotions aren't as well-known to history, for as far as we know she was not a diarist. However, Ronald's descriptions of her paint a vivid enough picture. She grieved the relationship just as he did, praying for him as he did for her. One cannot imagine the anxiety she must have felt over having potentially (though entirely accidentally) jeopardised her love's future.

Unfortunately, things were only going to get worse. Once again, these chance encounters were seen. Three days after the last time he saw Edith, Ronald received an angry letter from Father Francis. This time he did not mince words. Ronald had forfeit his chance to say goodbye to Edith at the station. All contact with her must cease completely and immediately. And if he disobeyed, Father Francis threatened the one thing that held as much value to Ronald as Edith: his university career. Ronald despaired, but complied. As he wrote in his diary, 'I owe all to Fr F. and so must obey.'[7]

And he did, with one small exception. But before that, although Edith would not jeopardise Ronald's future by attempting to visit, she managed to get a letter to him after news reached her of what had happened. 'Our hardest time of all has come,'[8] she wrote; heart-wrenching words considering what the pair had already endured, both as individuals and in their relationship. They truly seemed to love each other, so much so that even timid, rule-abiding Ronald could not go without one final small rebellion. On 2 March, Edith was to leave for Cheltenham. If a Birmingham resident had peered out of their window on that day, they might have seen a tall thin young man searching the streets, almost frantic. Nothing seems to ease his nerves, until, ironically on a street named Francis Road, a young lady passes him by on her bike.

This was to be the last time the pair saw each other for three whole years.

This period in Tolkien's life, both the relationship itself and the tumultuous fallout from it, had a profound effect on his writing. The women of Middle-Earth echo two figures in his life most of all: his mother Mabel and the love of his life, Edith. They are familiar with, and in some ways masters of, grief (Éowyn, Nienna, Galadriel), wise beyond their perceived years (Galadriel, Lúthien, Arwen), associated with nature and song (all of them) and occupy one of two roles: a wise, remote guardian (Galadriel, Nienna, Goldberry), or someone who will eventually wed one of the main characters (Éowyn, Lúthien, Arwen, Rosie Cotton). This is not so much a madonna/whore complex, as many male writers exhibit, but instead a 'distant ideal mother/love' dichotomy. One is not seen as greater or more important than the other, these heroines are not shamed for being, nor are they pitted against each other. However, only three are active participants in the story in which they feature, rather than guides or myths: Éowyn, Lúthien and Arwen. Interestingly, all three of these characters represent half of a heroic duo, the other half of which is always male (Éowyn and Merry (and later her husband Faramir), Lúthien and Beren and Arwen and Aragorn). Merry and Éowyn are the only heroic duo who do not marry, and are also the only heroic duo not of the same species (although Tolkien is ambiguous as to the origins of hobbits, it is clear that they are not human).

The Middle-Earth Tolkien created is one where women are only ever seen as proactive if they are part of a system involving men, either as their direct counterpart in the action or as a beneficiary of their care and wisdom. Unlike the men of Middle-Earth, who can have adventures without women, women cannot have adventures without men. However, there is one woman of Middle-Earth who stands apart from this, and who is perhaps Mabel Tolkien's final echo in the world.

At the beginning of *The Hobbit*, Bilbo Baggins, much like Tolkien, is orphaned from a young age, and has grown distant from one side of his family (the Sackville-Bagginses) due to their conniving nature. He lives alone comfortably off his wealth as a member of the Shire's landed gentry. It is established that he is happy with this comfortable, unadventurous life because he is a Baggins, and they are notorious stay-at-home sybarites. However, what motivates Bilbo to answer the call to adventure, and to even trust Gandalf the Grey, is the evocation of his mother: Belladonna Baggins (née Took). Belladonna is something of an ephemeral presence in the book; Gandalf knew her, and she had something of a reputation for being an outsider among the hobbits of the Shire, a free spirit whom Bilbo was close to. The weight that this relationship is given, without being described in detail, evokes Tolkien's relationship with his mother. He identified himself with hobbits frequently, and Bilbo specifically often; his love of smoking pipes, trees and the comforts of home, paired with his latent wild side and penchant for long meandering walks makes him an obvious parallel to Tolkien in his middle age and adage, as we shall see. But here, at the beginning of *The Hobbit*, Bilbo sits on the cusp of hobbit adulthood, comfy until a stranger, whom he would become very close to, takes him on an adventure, after invoking his deceased mother's thoughts and wishes. This is unlikely to be a direct, one-to-one synecdoche of Tolkien's feelings about Father Francis, his mother, and going to university (not least because Tolkien disliked stories that overt in their real life allegories), but it is certainly a symbolic one. Bilbo is motivated to find his true calling, that of risk and adventure, through a guardian who would grow to become as family to the hobbit, acting in what he perceives to be Bilbo's best interests, and considering the thoughts of Belladonna. Belladonna herself is still ephemeral; all we know is that the 'good folk' of the Shire did not hold her in as high regard as they did her husband, and there was some form of gossip about her. The Tooks themselves are far wilder than the Bagginses; their culture is slightly different to that of the Shire, they live communally in matriarchal compounds (crowded with activity and kin, much like the Suffield house that was Ronald's first English home).

Of course, there is one famous comparison between the women of Tolkien's life and their Middle-Earth counterparts: that of Edith and Lúthien, but that parallel was something Tolkien consciously created much later in life. However, there are also subtler shadows of cherished relationships (rather than distinct individuals) that Tolkien draws. His cousins, Mary and Marjorie Incledon, although they were instrumental and vital friends to Tolkien, and ignited his desire to create languages, are often overlooked in terms of whether or not they have counterparts in Middle-Earth, but I would posit that they do. Frodo Baggins, another hobbit orphaned young, and living with an older non-parental guardian, has two family members he is most close to: Peregrin 'Pippin' Took and Meriadoc 'Merry' Brandybuck, who are each other's first cousins, and Frodo's second and first cousins once removed, respectively. Where Frodo is reserved and even a touch depressed, which cannons into full-blown PTSD by the end of the events of *The Lord of the Rings*, Merry and Pippin are cheerful and playful, and usually have the best chance of lifting Frodo's mood. Their nicknames do not even read as masculine, and Merry's sounds almost identical to 'Mary'. What is particularly noticeable about the dynamic these three hobbits have is that Merry and Pippin, despite not being ringbearers, do not desert Frodo, even in his darkest times, on the grim adventure he must face. When he leaves all the Shire behind,

Samwise (whose inspirations were again more fully realised later), Merry and Pippin are the only parts of it that he can depend on and take with him through thick and thin.

The familial element of forgiveness and loyalty also plays a part in the depiction of Merry, but in particular Pippin. Pippin is the youngest, and (as the Tooks are famed to be) something of a wildcard who often gets the group into trouble with his impulsiveness and foolishness. However, he is not a character who is ever implied to be a burden that the hero needs to shed. Instead, the narrative focuses on how Pippin must undertake his own quest and grow as a person, which he does, and all the meanwhile Frodo and Merry forgive him his transgressions and love him all the same for them. Considering how much children's literature either treats mischievous characters as either dead weight to the hero or a sidekick for the hero to enjoy solely for comic relief, Pippin clearly has his own inner life, flaws and turmoil to overcome. He is not a flat character, he is a rounded-out member of Frodo's family, at times more insightful than Frodo. Is seems as if Mary and Marjorie, and certainly their creativity, playfulness and the value Ronald placed on their companionship growing up, allowed them to sneak into Middle-Earth after all.

To expand on an earlier theme, it is perhaps sadly telling how strongly the important women in his life who are reflected in his work as female characters have strong associations with grief. Nienna is the universal processor of it. Éowyn endures it. Arwen and Lúthien have it waiting in store for them because of who they love. Galadriel is fighting against it, and her arc comes to its end when she accepts it and leaves Middle-Earth for good. Belladonna is nothing but a reflected memory of someone lost, identified solely in relation to Gandalf and Bilbo's grief at having lost her at some unspecified point before *The Hobbit*. Tom Bombadil's wife, Goldberry, is identified as having lost her life as a river nymph in order to be with Tom Bombadil. Even Lobelia Sackville-Baggins, at first shown as a conniving unpleasant gossip, actualises into a brave defender of the Shire only after losing her beloved husband Lotho.

This strong connection to important women and grief is indicative of a truth about women in Tolkien's life. Simply put, they were the people he felt comfortable expressing his own deep feelings of grief to. Some of his earliest memories were of processing the loss of his father with his mother. He only fully found solace for losing her when he confided in Edith.

With Edith, he endured two world wars. Although grief is a pervading theme of both *The Hobbit* and *The Lord of the Rings*, it is only female characters who embody and express grief in this profound fundamental and vulnerable way. Perhaps this is indicative of how Tolkien lived his life; his male friends were who he laughed with, but his love and his female relations were who he felt comfortable crying around. Through this sheltered perspective, there is a kind of elevation to the mythic of female suffering in his works. Women lack emotional depth in comparison to the male characters, because they are so infinitely wise they cannot be flawed. Although more than mere receptacles for male sorrow, that is certainly a prevailing aspect of many of his women.

Indeed, this belief in such vastly different states between men and women was already starting to bloom in his adolescence, under Father Francis and the Catholic church's perception of gender. However, this gulf between his experiences and the private worlds of the women he knew would only deepen from here on out, for in December of 1910, after much hard study and applying himself, he got the news. He would be studying at Oxford University.

Chapter 6

A Holiday, and Isolation in Oxford

Before setting off to Oxford, there was to be one last great adventure for Ronald, one that would stay with him and find its ways into his works even years later. The call for adventure came from his aunt Jane Neave (who was close with both the boys) and Hilary. Now 17 years of age, Hilary was bright but even less suited to rigid academia than Ronald, and had no desire to continue down that path. But, like his brother, he felt a direct closeness to nature, and so from the age of 16 had pursued his dream of working the land. He was now working on Hurst Farm in Sussex, which belonged to the Brookes-Smiths. They were amiable employers, and fond of Hilary, and also close friends with Jane (likely from her time as a warden for St Andrews women's college), so when the family decided to go on a trip through Europe, Jane and Hilary were invited, and an invitation was even extended to Ronald.

The full party consisted of the Brookes-Smith family (husband and wife, their two teenage daughters and their 12-year-old son), two schoolmistresses for the children, a couple of other friends of the family whose names have been lost to time, and the Tolkien trio. And the trip was an ambitious one: a ship's passage from Harwich to Ostend (Belgium), then a series of trains from Cologne, Frankfurt and Munich (Germany), finally arriving at Austria's Innsbruck, near the Swiss border, where the meat of the holiday began. By both foot and by train, the party covered a huge distance to Interlaken in Switzerland, but from Interlaken onwards they were only to travel on foot, usually trekking along mountain paths and sometimes sleeping rough in barns along the way. In this manner they visited Lauterbrunnen, the vast Eiger and Mönch mountains, the Jungfrau and to Brig and the Rhone Valley, before returning to the mountains to visit the Aletsch Glacier. At the glacier, they stayed at a chalet, taking guided tours up to the glacier during the day.

The trip was as bold and potentially dangerous as it sounds, at one point Ronald came close to death. It was whilst they were touring the

Aletsch Glacier, which, after months of hot weather, was surrounded by melting ice, leading to stone screes and larger boulders falling down the mountainside. As the party were walking a narrow path (mountainside on one side and sheer drop on the other, naturally) one such boulder melted loose and bisected the party, falling between an elderly schoolmistress and Ronald. Fortunately, the schoolmistress had the presence of mind to cry out in warning as she leapt forwards out of the way, causing Ronald to freeze and the boulder to miss him by a foot. The experience so rattled him he went weak at the knees, which of course further prolonged his peril. Nevertheless, he recovered, and on the whole adored the trip and the landscape.

In fact, the locations on this trip are some of the few real world places that Tolkien acknowledged inspired his work. For example, in his adage, Tolkien wrote, 'I left the view of the Jungfrau with deep regret: eternal snow, etched as it seemed against eternal sunshine, and the Silberhorn sharp against the dark: the Silvertine (Celebdil) of my dreams.'[1] Celebdil is the southernmost of the Mountains of Moria surrounding the Dwarven ancestral city of Khazad-dûm. It is where the final battle between Gandalf and Durin's Bane the Balrog takes place, but perhaps more importantly, it is part of the sacred landscape of the Dwarves, where Durin (the first dwarf and first Dwarven king) first awoke on Middle-Earth. Indeed, you can hear something of teenage Ronald's excitement and marvel at the beauty of the Swiss landscape in Gimli's breathless awe and reverence at the sacred pool by the mountainside. Crucially, this is a moment of appreciation for the often spiritually moving power of nature as a respite from a tragedy (the group has just lost Gandalf, seemingly to death) and grief. Perhaps the conversation between Gimli and Frodo at Azanulbizar is a mirror of how Tolkien best processed his own grief from the life and love he lost in Birmingham, from his perspective at the time seemingly for good.

Further inspirations spring up along the path of this holiday; the Lauterbrunnen's name ('loud well/spring') bears etymological resonance to the Bruinen or River Loudwater surrounding Rivendell. It is a river Bilbo crosses on his travels and finds a place of staggering beauty and peacefulness to him just beyond, much like Tolkien's fondness for the Lauterbrunnen and all the wonderful sights he saw beyond it. And, of course, it would be remiss not to point out that the incident where Ronald

Tolkien almost wound up dying on the side of a glacier was the inspiration for the thunder-battle that waylays the party of Thorin Oakenshield as they cross the Misty Mountains, causing them to sleep in the cave which is Goblin-town's front porch. In general, the 'shape' of the trip, if you will, is extremely reminiscent of the plot structure of *The Hobbit*, starting in agricultural English countryside, a large party is formed, spearheaded by a single family to whom Ronald is a relative stranger. Together, they trek westwards a great distance, at times sleeping only where they can find a dry place to bed down, over and across stunning mountains and rivers, until they reach their goal of a place of relative luxury deep in the mountainside. Of course, it is unlikely that the line of Durin was based on the Brookes-Smiths, but an argument could certainly be made for the Tolkien boys' Aunt Jane, a worldly older woman with a fondness for the boys but a no-nonsense attitude, inspiring the mannerisms and mentality of Gandalf the Grey, who is at once Bilbo's mentor and friend, but also his frustrated teacher on more than one occasion.

Whether intentionally or not, this created a rite of passage trip for Tolkien, marking the bridge between his childhood and adulthood. And so, to Oxford he went. But alas, there were some caveats. He had been awarded as Open Classical Exhibition from Exeter College; not as valuable as the scholarship he sought (the exhibition being worth £60 a year), but it was a sign that he was capable of attending the college. King Edwards provided him a school-leaving bursary, and that meant that Father Francis was able to cover the rest. Although Father Francis had threatened to cut him off during the whole Edith debacle, he did not really have it in his heart to remain angry at the boy. He was incredibly proud of him for having got into Oxford, and wanted to support him through it as much as he was able.

In fact, everything from his finances to his trip to Oxford was an exercise in solidarity from those who believed in him, for it was Ronald's old school master Dickie Reynolds who drove the boy and his luggage to his rooms in his car, for such a trip would have been difficult by train, and that was all that Ronald could otherwise afford.

And so Ronald was thrust into the dreaming spires of Oxford. Though his own college, Exeter, was not considered as architecturally valuable or aesthetically pleasing by some, he was determined to love it. This was the opportunity of a lifetime for him and he knew it. Not to mention, although not a 'fashionable' college within the skewed priorities of the Oxford system, Exeter offered him many things he had not had for years: namely space and privacy. He not only had his own bedroom, but also his own living room, with views over a city which inspired him rather than depressed him, as Birmingham had. He had space to sit and read, take tea and daydream, or write; or space to fill with chatter and new friends, but on his own wishes, not by default.

Although he did not know it yet, he was in fact quite fortunate to have landed at Exeter College, and not one of the more prestigious, old-money, traditional colleges. The University of Oxford, much like its rival, the University of Cambridge, had deeply classist institutional roots, dedicated to preserving the power of a few upper-class 'elites' over offering an accessible education for anyone who would flourish there. Although the scholarship system did elevate some students who otherwise would not have the opportunity to study there, it was the connections old money students had and made which allowed them to slide easily into prosperous careers or even positions of political power within the UK. The upper classes maintained their hold on the resources with an iron grip, and in many subjects to make something of oneself, even if gifted, this unique opportunity was (and remains to this day) an uphill struggle for those who were not born into power.

Similarly, social benefits, or even socialising, were held away from students outside of upper class and aristocratic backgrounds. If Ronald had ended up in one of the dreamier spires he would likely not have loved Oxford as he did. However, Exeter College was nowhere near the top of this collegiate hierarchy. As such, even its students from more privileged backgrounds were less exclusionary, and Tolkien – middle class, amiable and eager to throw his hat into any fun going as he was – quickly made friends. However, this is not to say that Exeter College was truly iconoclastic; Tolkien may have been less well-off than the elites, but he was still middle class as opposed to working class. One wonders what his university days would have been like if his accent had not been quite so received... Nonetheless, Tolkien himself made friends with the other scholarship students, and the wealthier students, and anyone who was interested in giving his lanky, passionate young man a chance to enthuse about whatever caught his attention in that particular moment.

However, privately, very privately, he was still grieving the loss of his relationship with Edith. Even during his happiest times at Oxford, he pined for her. It seems as if that what he was missing was the companionship of those who could understand and allow him to voice his depression when he was with them. Without Edith, or the TCBS, he had companionship for fun and hijinks, but no-one to truly *talk* to openly, as he desired. This was not to say that he wasn't enjoying himself, he was, but there was still a fundamental lack that he felt throughout his time at Oxford.

As for Edith, she was also grieving their separation, but also flourishing. Life with the solicitor and his wife (the Jessops) was far better than the life to be had under Mrs Faulkner's roof. She had her independence, and the security of a roof over her head with kind folk who supported her. In fact, she grew so close to the Jessops that she took to calling them auntie and uncle, although they were not blood relations. They loved her in turn; though Mr Jessop was sometimes a cantankerous sort, his grumpiness was never directed at Edith, whom he was fond of, but instead at the world. Mrs Jessop was a complete contrast to her husband: a sweet and openly kind woman, who was inclined to go out of her way to spoil Edith when Mr Jessop was in a particularly bad mood.

The house was much quieter than 34 Duchess Road; there were few visitors save for the parish vicar and a few of the Jessops' elderly friends, but Edith was not lonely. Aside from the family she had built for herself with the Jessops, one of her dear school friends, Molly Field, lived nearby with her family, so she did not want for company. Furthermore, she even had an active social life; she was an active and regularly attending member of her Anglican church, and even joined the Primrose League. This was an organisation dedicated to popularising the ideals and politics of the Conservative Party throughout the class system of the UK. Their symbol, the primrose, was chosen for the fact that it was Benjamin Disraeli's favourite flower, and their somewhat Orwellian motto was *Imperium et libertas* (Latin for 'Control and freedom'). That Edith was drawn to this political organisation reflects the somewhat contradictory position she had at the time within England's class system; she owned land, and was a member of the middle classes, but she was poor, illegitimate and what little societal status she had was entirely reliant on the benevolence of socially conservative people like the Jessops, and the Faulkners. Although she had been perilously close to destitution many times in her life, she was not working class, and did not have an understanding of how working class voices should be upheld within politics, as from their own community rather than preached down to them through the upper classes.

Additionally, and crucially for Edith, the Primrose League was one of the few political parties in England, by some accounts even the first in England, to offer equal power and responsibilities to white middle-class women as they offered to white middle-class men.[2] In order to have control over her own political voice, and to even have a political voice, Edith had one of two options: either to be completely radical and join a Suffragist movement, and almost certainly lose her home and security, or join an organisation like the Primrose League. And so, through the Primrose League, Edith became very politically active, attending the fêtes the group held for the community alongside going to Conservative Party meetings.

Aside from this social freedom, Edith found something even more important for her well-being and happiness in the Jessop's home. Unlike Mrs Faulkner, their love for music was not superficial. She was allowed and able to flourish as the musician she could be. She practised her piano every day, and even started to take lessons on the organ, eventually playing it for her parish church. In many ways, her talents were being encouraged and supported in Cheltenham just as Ronald's were in Oxford. As harsh as it had seemed, the impetus for them to leave Birmingham had done them the world of good. Edith even managed to say as much to Ronald. At Easter, with the asked for and (grudgingly) granted permission of Father Francis, Ronald was allowed to write to Edith, who wrote back, affirming that she was very happy in Cheltenham and that 'all that horrid time at Duchess Road seems only a dream now'.[3] Tolkien was reconnecting with his languages as Edith was with her music.

However, this is not to endorse their separation, or say that it had a wholly positive effect. In fact, this three year period of separation had a deeply deleterious effect on Tolkien's writing and maybe even his psyche, one that would dog him for decades and almost ruin his relationship with the love of his life. Going from Birmingham, where his close friends outside of Edith were the TCBS from his all-boys' school and his younger brother, where one of the last messages Father Francis had given him in a fit of pique over their falling out was that spending time with women was frivolous and evil, he pitched into the academia of Oxford. And Oxford was even worse; although they did admit female students, they were sequestered away in all-female colleges, and the environment was all-male to the active exclusion of female influences; the etiquette and social hierarchy of a boys' club was preserved in full. This, combined with the sense of self-importance Oxfordian students were actively encouraged to adopt, that they were the next generation of thinkers and power brokers and the world should treat them accordingly (regardless of their abilities or morality) led to the development of a toxic mindset. Women were invisible, and if they fought to be seen and heard their thoughts could not possibly be as important as the Oxfordian men.

And bit by bit, Ronald adopted this flawed mindset, not intentionally, but through osmosis of the company he kept and enjoyed. His heart may have belonged to Edith, but his body was in Oxford, and the worst parts of its system were beginning to claim his mind. As Edith was establishing herself as an intelligent and valued voice in her community, Ronald was unconsciously learning how to disregard her.

It is saddening to see a man of that era, whose unique literary voice was shaped by the important women in his life, become clouded and distorted by the entrenched cultural misogyny of the time, but to gloss over that in his biography would be grossly disingenuous. From this point on, the influence of the women and girls who had meant so much to him existed in this idealised but remote bubble in his head, away from his man-friends and their important thoughts and creative fervour. Mabel became a remote martyr, her defiant and iconoclastic sisters Jane and May softened in his memory to wise kindly motherly figures and nothing more. His Tolkien aunt who told him the fantastical stories of his heritage was worse remembered than the men in her tales. When he thought of creating languages, he did not think of Mary and Marjorie, but instead of Christopher Wiseman encouraging him in his solo efforts. And finally, Edith, his equal before their separation, became a romantic ideal, softened, no longer a person, in his lovelorn mind. She became so much this remote ideal that he kept a diary of his failings at Oxford for her, as if she could absolve him as a saint would.

In many ways this is a damning indictment of structure of academia of the day; to pursue it was to enter an institute where misogyny was so ingrained and pervasive that it distorted the thoughts of even those with a large number of women and girls they looked up to and respect in their history. One wonders how many 'great thinkers' could have actually achieved greatness if their perspective hadn't been so flattened.

The impact of going into adulthood in the exclusively male space is wrought throughout his Middle-Earth books. Women very much have a 'separate but equal' role in Middle-Earth society. As discussed in the previous chapter, they are often brave, capable, extremely powerful and wise, but they are not the heroes of the story, nor is their presence expected at any point in the adventures of Bilbo and Frodo. The world of Middle-Earth is set up as if women are an optional extra to life, either impossible towering figures of myth or ghosts on the corners of family histories. Many of the women of Middle-Earth are noted by their absence. One prominent example of this is Dís, Thorin Oakenshield's sister and the mother of Fili and Kili. By the end of *The Hobbit*, she is the last surviving member of the Line of Durin, Thorin and his nephews (her only children) having perished in the final battle. And yet we never meet her. Her perspective on the events of the book, her brother's quest, her children's involvement, is valuable and unique, yet she is only ever mentioned in passing; a name on a family tree. This is particularly striking given that her arc, one of processing a lifetime of grief, is a subject dear to Tolkien's heart which he explores with many other characters, and yet Dís is silenced by the text. One could even take this line of questioning further and ask why she wasn't a member of Thorin's Company. It would not be an issue of physical capability (not that it would with any female character but this is often the first step on the ladder of bad faith questions); Dwarves are one of the few species of Middle-Earth that are explicitly mentioned as having low sexual dimorphism. Dwarven women are just as strong, sturdy, bearded and capable at crafts as Dwarven men, and yet none of them appear in the stories of Middle-Earth.

Hobbit women appear either as deceased rebels (Belladonna, Sméagol's unnamed grandmother), redeemable crones (Lobelia) or love interests with barely anything documented about them (Rosie Cotton). The last example is particularly egregious. Rosie is Sam's future wife, and even though Sam is a crucial character in *The Lord of the Rings*, whose inner life, motivations, and relatives are given many words, Rosie is the pretty girl waiting at home to be married to Sam, a nurturing and romantic figure, scarcely allowed to be more than a face in the crowd.

Among the Elves and Men are the most active female characters in the stories; Galadriel, Lúthien, Arwen and Éowyn are active participants in the story, but they are not Fellowship members, nor (with the exception of the remote, deified Galadriel) are they allowed to escape the narrative without becoming the love interest of a male hero.

Tolkien's time in Oxford left an ideal clear in his mind: that good women were either saintly mothers or love interests, but never heroes in their own right.

Tolkien's time in Oxford was also not initially focused on studies. Like a lot of students, especially ones from families that didn't go to university, at first Ronald was swept up by the spectacle of young men able to run wild without consequence. However, unlike most of the 'poor scholars' as they were known, in his first year he got involved. Regularly. In his own words from the time, here is an evening's entertainment:

> 'We "ragged" the town and the police and the proctors all together for about an hour. Geoffrey and I "captured" a bus and drove it up to Cornmarket making various unearthly noises followed by a mad crowd of mingled varsity and "townese". It was chockfull of undergrads before it reached the Carfax. There I addressed a few stirring words to a huge mob before descending and removing to the "maggers memugger" or the Martyr's Memorial where I addressed the crowd again. There were no disciplinary consequences of all this!'[4]

As one might expect, his grades began to slip. He was reading Classics, and thoroughly bored of the subject, finding his tutor dry and the languages passé. This was a boy who had been comfortable enough with Latin and Greek to fluently debate in them at school (Latin was expected of the curriculum, the Greek was not) and even back then he sometimes comfortably spoke Gothic and Saxon in his debates, so now the whole enterprise seemed terribly dull to him. Aside from disruptive rowdiness with the idle rich around Oxford, he also threw himself into extracurricular activities. He was still an avid rugby player (never reaching huge success on the college team but enthusiastic nonetheless), a member of Stapleton (the debating society), and even founded his own clubs in his first year. Comprised mainly of freshmen such as himself, they read papers aloud, held debates and informal discussions, and had extremely extravagant club dinners. Fittingly, as his club activities seemed to be comprised of his favourite things, Ronald called them the Apolausticks, meaning 'those devoted to self-indulgence'. And of course, he was still dedicated to creating his languages in his spare time.

Fortunately, his special subject – Comparative Philology – brought him into the path of a professor who inspired him and motivated him to apply himself to the subjects he loved so much: Joseph 'Joe' Wright.

Professor Wright was an anomaly in Oxford: a working-class Yorkshireman who retained his accent with pride and cared not for the extravagance of his wealthy peers. His journey into academia was also something straight out of fiction in its remarkable climb from poverty to the top of his field. He was sent to work in a woollen mill from age 6, with no schooling and completely illiterate. However, when he was 15 years old he grew envious of his literate colleagues (specifically their ability to read the newspapers) so he taught himself to read. He found himself to have a knack for it, and be a fast learner, so he sent himself to night school to study French and German, and taught himself Latin and maths at the same time, pouring over his books until two in the morning, before getting up for work at five. By the age of 18 he felt obligated to pass on his knowledge to his co-workers, and set up a night school in his bedroom in his widowed mother's cottage. Admission was tuppence a week. Three years later, he had amassed enough to enrol at Heidelberg University in Germany for a term. He travelled to Heidelberg by taking a boat to Antwerp in Belgium, and then walking the ninety-hour or so rest of the journey!

In Heidelberg he discovered his love of philology. Back in England he attended the Yorkshire College of Science (now the University of Leeds), paying for his tuition by working as a schoolmaster. A former pupil recalled: 'with a piece of chalk [he would] draw illustrative diagrams at the same time with each hand, and talk while he was doing it!'[5] Eventually he took his doctorate in Heidelberg. By the time he returned to England a second time, he had studied Old Bulgarian, Old English, Old and Middle High German, Gothic, Lithuanian, Old Norse, Russian, Sanskrit, and Old Saxon. He secured a position at Oxford and swiftly rose to be the Deputy Professor of Comparative Philology. Whilst in Oxford, he worked on many books, including his English Dialect Dictionary, which is still a unique and valuable preservation of dialects and culture. The massive six-volume tome initially had to be self-financed into publication, but fortunately its importance was later recognised and Professor Wright celebrated for the wonderful scholar he was.

Now based in Oxford, he fell in love there: with fellow philologist and academic authoress Mary Elizabeth Lea, who was also a former student of his. They married and had two children, but sadly both died in childhood. Throughout his academic career, he touched the lives of many of the great writers of the nineteenth and twentieth century; Thomas Hardy was a correspondent of his, and Virginia Woolf hugely respected and admired him, even basing the character of Mr Brook in *The Pargiters* on him.

By the time Tolkien was his pupil, Professor Wright – now the Professor of Comparative Philology – was an apple-cheeked portly man with a well-combed stiff white brush of a beard. He taught male and female students alike, and invited them all to his house for great Sunday teas, where he and Elizabeth spoiled them all with huge slices of cake.

He was a kindly man, and one highly aware of the shortcomings of Oxford University; he once told Ronald that Oxford was not 'a place of learning' as Ronald had suggested, but was instead 'a factory! And what's it making? I'll tell you. It's making fees.'[6] Decades later Ronald admitted to his son Michael that Joe had been completely right, he had simply refused to see it for as long as possible, preferring to dismiss this sound advice as the words of 'an old vulgarian…'. But most importantly for Ronald, he was an excellent teacher: one especially good at pushing talented students who were perhaps not applying themselves as much as they could.

For Ronald, his lessons were a much-needed awakening. He had come to Oxford with a broader knowledge of languages than any of his peers, and so had been happy to sink into complacency, but a few lessons with Professor Wright and he quickly realised he had so much to learn, but more importantly that he wanted to learn it.

One piece of advice Ronald found easier to swallow than Joe's words on the corporate nature of Oxford was his words on study: 'Go in for Celtic, lad; there is money in it.'[7] However, Joe probably meant modern Welsh, but Ronald – ever the traditionalist – saw this as carte blanche to get stuck into medieval Welsh, which he found to be just as delightful as he'd hoped as a child. He adored the aesthetics of the language, both the sounds and the spellings, and from there he bounded into his other childhood mystery language, Finnish, with aplomb.

His focus on studying ancient literature was for perhaps more prosaic reasons than the pursuit of childhood passions and to confuse his mentor. If he was only ever studying dead languages, then it would never be deemed necessary for him to have to travel to where the language was spoken to enrich his studies, and travelling (much like seemingly everything else in Oxford, he soon found) cost a lot more than he'd hoped it to. Although he seemed to fit in with the upper-class students, he was still a poor scholar, and as Oxford was designed and priced to cater to students with inherited wealth to burn (sometimes literally, as in the case of the still-active today covert clubs such as the Bullingdon Club). Simply put: Ronald didn't have those funds. He loved having his two rooms and his fireplace but he had to furnish them beyond the bare essentials if he was to entertain guests. It was a novel delight to have meals provided by the college but those food bills became awfully long. As many young students did, Tolkien rapidly found his impression of university changing from an idyll of youthful excess and destruction, to a seat of learning, to a black hole which sapped all his money. The bills piled up and up, as did Tolkien's worries, for there was more than just personal strain on the horizon.

Chapter 7

On the Eve of War

He had settled into a comfortable rhythm at Oxford, frivolities with friends, private languages, diaries of his missteps, and hard work under the watchful eye of Professor Wright for Comparative Philology. But by the end of 1912, that was all about to change, under his own wishes.

That year, he spent Christmas with the Incledons in Birmingham. As was traditional, the family put on little plays for each other as part of the entertainment. Ronald, who in later life would declare he hated drama, penned one of the plays for that season. Unbeknownst to the Incledons, Ronald's nonsense play would have more truth in it than fiction. Called *The Bloodhound, the Chef, and the Suffragette*, it was the tale of a highly decorated professor (a Joseph Quilter, played by Ronald) who also led a double life as a private detective. He's on the trail of the Suffragette Gwendoline Goodchild, a lost heiress, who plans to remain lost for the next two days. For Gwendoline has fallen in love with a penniless student in her lodgings, and will only be free to marry him after her twenty-first birthday in two days' time. Whilst there are obvious parallels to his situation with Edith (he was turning 21 less than ten days after Christmas, after all), another striking bit of real-world inspiration for his play is Professor Wright, who he clearly held in such high regard that he could imagine him as a vigilante of sorts on the side of his work.

Christmas came and went, and on 3 January 1913, Ronald turned 21. He had stayed up the night before until midnight, and at the minute he was 21 he penned a letter to Edith, declaring his love for her over again and asking when they could be married.[1]

When Edith wrote back, the response felt like a punch in the gut. She was glad to hear from him, but was already engaged. Her school-friend Molly had a brother, George Field, who had fallen for her in these three long years apart.

Ronald considered his options. Edith had been kept a secret from everyone close to him save for Father Francis. Not the TCBS, nor his Oxford friends, nor his family knew of her existence. He could save face and let things be and no-one would be any the wiser. But Ronald would not, could not, let their time in Duchess Road be a mere memory, nor the three years during which he pined and diaried for her. He had to meet with her and make his case. And so, on 8 January, he boarded a train bound for Cheltenham.

From Edith's perspective, the three years had been a hugely positive period of support, change and growth in her life, but her faith in her relationship with Ronald dwindled year after year. Where was he? She had certainly thought him bright enough to get into Oxford as was his dream, did he succeed? If so, what was to stop him from writing to her at least once or twice a year, to let her know that she was still in his thoughts, as he was in hers? How would his guardian even know? Now that Edith was away from Birmingham she was flourishing and pushing the limits of her newfound independence, why wasn't Ronald doing the same?

And so doubt crept into her mind, no doubt exacerbated by the depression she too had keenly felt since childhood. Had Ronald forgotten her and his promises? Had their time together meant so little? She was in the precarious position where she could not simply write back and ask, that was something easily discoverable by Father Francis, and could lead to further pain for Ronald and perhaps her being completely forbidden from him ever again, but she agonised over why Ronald could not write to her. She had stayed at the same address for three years, he could find her if he wished.

All the while, every other aspect of her life proved fun and fulfilling. She had great friends, performed her music, exercised her political voice, and was now close with not just Molly but now the whole Field family. And Molly's brother George was quite the gentleman. Although Edith had both male and female friends, George was the only young man she knew, as her social circle was so closely tied to Auntie and Uncle Jessop. He was a farmer, so plied a secure and reliable trade, and he was sweet and kind, and clearly quite in love with her. Edith certainly reciprocated feelings of fondness and friendship, but seemingly not romantic love. When she spoke of him (and when she wrote of him in her reply to Ronald), she described him as good husband material: 'suitable' rather than desirable.

But at the same time, Ronald was not there, and may never be. She was now nearly 24, and felt 'on the shelf'.[2] However, Ronald's letter changed everything. Her response was not a discouragement, nor was it a simple statement of fact, it was an intentional invitation for Ronald to fight for her. 'I had begun to doubt you, Ronald, and to think you would cease to care for me,' she wrote, all the while describing her engagement to George Field in the most utilitarian terms.

So on 8 January, she set out to Cheltenham train station, to meet Ronald on the platform. They walked together, and found a place to sit (under the railway viaduct) to talk to each other for the first time in years. And as they talked, the years of separation slipped away. They became certain of their love for each other. By the end of the day, Edith had resolved to break off her engagement to George, and to marry Ronald.

Although they were both delighted, they resolved to remain cautious, and keep the engagement secret for now, save for a few people who must know. Edith wrote to George explaining her feelings, breaking off the engagement and sending back his ring as soon as possible. Understandably, George was completely heartbroken, and George and Molly's family was furious. But after a while that storm quelled, later, to the point when it was no longer worth talking about, they all became friends once more.

But Ronald had one person he felt he had to tell: Father Francis. Even thinking about this made Ronald a bag of nerves. Although he was no longer beholden to him as his legal guardian, Father Francis was still financially helping him throughout his studies at Oxford. And, of course, Ronald cared about his mentor deeply. This news could cause a rift between them that would never heal. However, he worried in vain; Father Francis wrote back, and although he was not exactly overjoyed, he was accepting and respectful of Ronald and Edith's decision, and loving of both Ronald and Edith. But his worries were not entirely misplaced, for some of them were practical, and would be real tribulations the sweethearts would face.

They had little money between them, for one, and Ronald's prospects were poor and would remain so until he graduated, and even then he would need a respectable grade. Engagement to Edith had to be a wake-up call for him to knuckle down and really work hard when he returned to Oxford. Now he had to build a future not just for himself, but for Edith.

He returned to Oxford for the new term filled with 'a bursting happiness',[3] but he needed more than that to sustain him through the next term. For in six weeks' time were his Honour Moderations, the first set of exams he needed to complete to earn his Classics degree. Up until now he had been something of a slacker, so, like many students before and since, he crammed what should have been four terms' worth of study and learning into a few short weeks.

To his credit, he did remarkably well, considering. He was struggling to wake up in the mornings (probably due to still staying up late and working on his languages, though he wouldn't hear of that explanation, preferring instead to blame the Oxfordian damp), and struggling even harder with the impositions of limiting his social life. But he pulled it altogether, and managed to get a Second Class (a First being the highest possible grade). Although Exeter College was disappointed with his results (it prefers all of its scholarship students to obtain Firsts) there was one part of his results that both Ronald and the college could be incredibly proud of: a pure alpha (practically perfect paper) in Comparative Philology. Given that both his results and his heart seemed to be drifting further and further from Classics day by day, Exeter College 'encouraged' him to pursue philology, and suggested he switch to the English school. Though it should be specified that this was not out of the kindness of their heart; Exeter and all of the colleges were results-driven first and foremost.

Nonetheless, this would seem like a perfect fit for him, so Tolkien took them up on the offer. At the time the English Language and Literature school was firmly divided. On the one hand, the philologists and medievalists who considered any literature post-Chaucer nowhere near complex or worthy enough to merit degree study, and on the other hand, modernists who studied from Chaucer to the nineteenth century and thought the medievalists to be regressive pedants. The school contained both specialisations to provide the students with a more rounded curriculum and grounding in the English language, but of course both parties felt hard done by by this choice. Tolkien was bound to fit right in with the philologists, though at first he found his tutor Kenneth Sisam somewhat uninspiring. Kenneth Sisam was a quiet man, a soft-spoken New Zealander only four years older than Tolkien himself, a sharp contrast from the advanced years and commanding presence of Professor Wright. However, Sisam was diligent and earnest, and a true scholar in his field, extremely passionate about his work. Eventually, he earned Tolkien's respect and the younger man grew very fond of him. The trajectory of their relationship mirrors that of Tolkien's with his course; at first he was certain that there was not enough on the syllabus that he did not know already to satiate him for another two years and change, but over time he realised that he had so much further to go as a scholar. The translation and fluency standards of the school were much higher than his self-imposed ones, and he also had to dedicate his time to the literature side of the course.

As such, he spent far more time studying and far less partying than he had in the Classics department. Perhaps this was also a sign of an advancing maturity; he had a fiancée now and his degree choices were more focused on what his eventual career would be in the end. He was looking to the future.

On the subject of the future, specifically his future with Edith, some months into their engagement they hit a road bump. In order to be married, Edith had decided that she would convert to Catholicism, but merely wished to delay her conversion for a few months, at least until they had made their engagement public. Ronald would not hear of it, unloading a tirade against the Anglican faith – which Edith still believed and practised at the time, in a letter to her. '[It is] a pathetic and shadowy medley of half-remembered traditions and mutilated beliefs.'[4]

Edith was understandably hurt by this. Not only had the Anglican church supported her whilst she had been forced to leave Birmingham, but she also had an a place in her local parish community. It was her connection to her friends and her faith, and of course her organ music performances. Asking her to cast this off was as light as asking Ronald to discard one of his private languages. Furthermore, converting now would put her in real danger. Uncle Jessop was staunchly anti-papist, and there was every possibility that converting would result in Edith losing her home and her found family.

But Ronald was stubborn, and fell back upon a great misunderstanding of a tragedy in his early life. The argument he fired back to Edith was that his mother had been persecuted and suffered greatly for her faith, then why couldn't Edith also endure? This epitomises the sexism of Ronald's thinking at the time; he had forgotten that Mabel's persecution was something she (and he and Hilary) had wanted to avoid at any costs, and over the years he had processed that trauma of watching her suffer as martyrdom, necessary for her faith and part of why he held her in such elevated regard. It was not that Mabel had been a good mother and wonderful teacher, it was that she had suffered to provide. In Ronald's mind, women's importance and worthy work now had to be borne from suffering.

One wonders if there would have been any change in his resolve if his engagement had been known about by his family, or if he was still in regular correspondence with Father Francis. It seems doubtful that his aunt May, whose own faith was crushed by her husband all those years ago, would have let him endanger Edith in this way without giving him more than a piece of her mind. Even Father Francis' own faith was not rooted in the need to suffer, and perhaps he could have offered a calmer perspective, and maybe contextualised some of what Mabel endured at the time that Ronald was sheltered from in his youth.

Alas, this was not the case, and so Edith reluctantly obeyed his wishes. Unsurprisingly, her worst fears were realised. Uncle Jessop hit the roof, and this time there was nothing his wife could do to calm him. His instructions were clear: Edith must leave the house as soon as she found alternative accommodation.

Having caused this upset, Ronald had no way to resolve this. He submitted the idea that Edith could move to Oxford (though of course she would not be allowed to stay in his student rooms) and she immediately shot him down. Perhaps she was not fond of Oxford, or perhaps she wanted some distance and separation from Ronald in case their engagement fell apart. Additionally, she did not have enough funds to rent a place alone. Molly Field had no desire to move out of her home (and was not currently on the best of terms with Edith at any rate), so Edith turned to the one person she had truly been able to rely on her whole life: Jennie Grove. Jennie was glad to move in with her once more, and so the two women eventually settled on Warwick as the place they wished to live.

They found temporary rooms there and Ronald joined them there to visit and to help with the finding of a permanent home. Whilst there, they did have some fun times; Ronald and Edith punted down the Avon together, which they both loved for its scenery, and they also attended Benediction at the local Roman Catholic church. They came away joyous, for they were both deeply religious people and this was the first time they had ever been able to openly attend church together. However, there was work to be done. Edith and Jennie needed a home, and Ronald needed to help find one before he had to return to his studies. But it was debatable as to whether or not his presence helped more than hindered. Afflicted with the wretched Oxbridge perception that his thoughts were noble and his occupations should be noble, he saw everything else as a tawdry waste of his time, including helping his fiancée find a home after he had put her in the position of facing homelessness.

Understandably, Edith did not take his change in attitude lightly. Her life and interests were being seen as trivial, and she wouldn't have it. Their time together was no longer always blissful smooth sailing, but often marred with arguments. Both of them had changed and matured, but where Edith had expanded her horizons, Ronald had narrowed his. He was no longer used to domesticity and female company, and worse, did not see that he should have to partake in the former.

Nonetheless, eventually Edith and Jennie found and moved into their house, and Ronald returned to Oxford, his engagement still intact. He and Edith's letters at the time are loving but a mutual frustration bubbled under the surface. Now they no longer understood each other as they did when they were in Duchess Road. Ronald was dismissive of Edith's interests, and, from Edith's perspective, Ronald's sole preoccupation with books and language was selfish when there was a whole world out there that he was ignoring.

In large part, this rift which grew between them at this time was Ronald's fault. He insisted on keeping his academic life separate from Edith. This left her with no through-way into the most important things in his life, including what he was spending most of his days doing. However, they stuck by each other, and Edith gave Ronald the space he apparently now needed to pursue his passions.

From Warwick, Tolkien travelled to Paris, where, in order to earn a little cash whilst travelling, he had secured a summer tutoring job for three Mexican boys who were travelling with their aunts. The aunts and one of the boys spoke very little English, so Ronald was forced to rely on his rudimentary and now fairly rusty Spanish, as well as his even more rusty and cobwebbed French to get by. In spite of his xenophobic views on France, he found that he enjoyed Paris very much, though the city did not quell his feelings towards the French, and he wrote to Edith from Paris of how he despised the Frenchmen around him for all number of reasons, including but not limited to it being common practice at the time to spit in the street. From there the family travelled on to Brittany, which excited Ronald for there survived among the Bretons an archaic language very similar to Welsh. However, he discovered that the location they were to be staying in, Brittany's Dinard, was in fact a touristy seaside resort, which he despised. Ronald was already in a foul mood when things became awful. He was walking with one of the boys and the eldest of the two aunts when a car mounted the pavement, running her down. Ronald helped get her back to their hotel, but she succumbed to internal injuries, dying a few hours later. Ronald was thoroughly shaken from his ill-tempered malaise and forced to take responsibility for three young boys under the direst of circumstances. The younger aunt, who was distraught at the sudden loss of her sister, had to find a way to get her body back to Mexico, and the bureaucracy of it plus the language barrier, not to mention the distress of it all, meant that that occupied much of her mind. It was up to Ronald to get the boys back to England (where they had other relatives) himself, which he just about managed, swearing to Edith in writing that he would never take such a job again unless he was severely desperate and impoverished.

Naturally, he returned for the autumn term of 1913 deeply shaken by the experience, but fortunately he was to be less alone, for G.B. Smith had now made it to Oxford. This made the Oxbridge split of TCBS boys completely even: for Christopher and Rob were at Cambridge. So life settled back into a routine once more; Ronald studied, socialised in Oxford (especially with G.B. Smith, who was very dear to him), and wrote to Edith, visiting her in Warwick when he could. Meanwhile, as the months passed, Ronald realised that he would have to tell his friends about his engagement. He and Edith had decided that they would announce their betrothal after Edith's confirmation, which was fast approaching. This was making him almost as nervous as writing to Father Francis had. In particular he was struggling to tell the TCBS, feeling that they might take it as a betrayal that he had had this great love affair whilst they had been at school together and had been none the wiser. When he wrote to them all he did not even mention Edith by name. However, he needn't have worried; Christopher, Rob and Geoffrey all wrote back expressing only their warmest wishes. GB was even astute enough to reassure Ronald that this had in no way lowered his standing in the TCBS, and that he would likely always be one of them.

And so Edith was instructed into Catholicism by one Father Murphy of the Warwick parish, who was not as enthusiastic a teacher as Mabel or any of the Oratory were. Tolkien would blame much of Edith's failure to grasp what he saw as the true nature of the Catholic faith on his poor teaching for years to come, whilst also not explaining himself further to Edith; his own faith was tangled with his feelings about Mabel so he struggled to express it. Regardless, Edith followed her own path through Catholicism, and was received into the church on 8 January 1914, on the first anniversary of her and Ronald's reunion. After that, she and Ronald were officially betrothed by Father Murphy, and she took her first communion and confession, finding a profound religious joy in the act. This renewed her spiritual connection to the Catholic church, and for a while she tried to turn that into a social connection, as her old Anglican parish had been. She regularly attended Mass and threw herself into the parish social scene, but it simply wasn't the same as Cheltenham. The church was neither as welcoming nor as close-knit, so she kept finding excuses not to attend.

Although she still found Warwick as beautiful a city as when she first moved there, she began to slide into depression once more. Without a church community her entire social circle consisted of Jennie Grove and Ronald (when he was visiting). But Ronald had changed and grown distant and dismissive, and she and Jennie loved each other, but still bickered now and then. She had only enough money to occasionally go out to a concert, or the theatre, and her new parish had no need of her organ-playing skills, although she had volunteered them. She did have a piano, and could play for hours on end, but now it felt different, hollow somehow. Now that she knew she would never be a professional musician, that instead she was to become a housewife and mother, her passion dimmed, and sometimes the thing just made her sad.

It seemed as if the star-crossed lovers' relationship might not last; Ronald's conditions on Edith had made her isolated and miserable and he was becoming frustrated with what he saw as her preoccupation with trivial matters, but all that was soon to change, and not for positive reasons.

On 4 August, 1914, England declared war on Germany. And Ronald, Edith, Geoffrey, Christopher and Rob's lives were all about to change forever.

The first part of the war machine to activate was the appeal for soldiers, famously led by Kitchener. The pressure felt upon young men, especially those who called themselves nationalists and patriots, of which Tolkien was one, to join up was immense. England had yet to shake its colonial mindset from the Victorian era, and so war was not seen as something that could be tragic or disturbing or traumatising for its participants, it was instead an opportunity to show your valour for king and country. Scores of Tolkien's peers joined up. His younger brother Hilary joined up, enlisting as a bugler. And Tolkien's family waited for him to tell them the 'good' news that he was going to war.

But it would not come. Tolkien wanted to finish his studies, and was eager for a First Class, which would allow him to pursue academia as a career, as was his wish. And so the pressuring began. At the time young men were put under huge social pressure to enlist, up to and including complete strangers dropping white feathers in their laps as a symbol of cowardice if they were out in public. Both the Tolkiens and the Suffields tried over and over to wear him down and force him to enlist. The only person he could rely on was Edith, who stuck by him through familial shaming and also did not want him risking his life and limb on foreign fields. By now Ronald's family was seeing him as the problem child; first he announces his engagement to an older woman, and now he refuses to fight.

However, eventually they were mollified, when Ronald discovered a scheme at the university whereby students could train for the army whilst they finished their degree. Furthermore, all was not lost; although almost everyone he knew was now gone, he had one friend still there, with whom he now lived in digs: a Colin Cullis, who could not go to war on account of his poor health. Even better, G.B. Smith was still in Oxford, as he was awaiting commission. He had signed up for the Lancashire Fusiliers, which made Ronald determined to join them too once he had graduated, ideally in the same regiment and battalion, such was their bond. A few days into term, drill training started in the University Parks with the Officers' Training Corps, which he found he enjoyed, believing the early morning routine on top of his coursework kept him more awake, allowing him to avoid what he called the 'Oxford sleepies'.

Chapter 8

Shells Burst

The routine of drills, socialising, and studying went on as it did, the war seeming nothing but an abstract remote occurrence in Tolkien's mind, something that he would have to deal with eventually but currently had little impact on his life. The biggest event in his immediate future was a rare in-person meeting with all of the TCBS.

At the beginning of the Christmas holiday, Tolkien, Wiseman, Gilson and Smith descended on the Wiseman family's home (the rest of the family having moved south) to reconnect and discuss their passions. On the cusp of a seismic world event, in universities that would give them access to connections and knowledge that could put the world at their feet, they felt like they could, or would, be a driving force for the world. Wiseman said they felt 'four times their intellectual size'[1] together.[2] Tolkien even compared them to the Pre-Raphaelite Brotherhood, which his friends roundly mocked for taking it too far. But together they did feel a freedom to discuss their creative work in a serious manner, and experiment with forms of expression they perhaps didn't have the confidence to pursue on their own. Ronald found this extremely liberating, a welcome break from the pent-up stresses and frustrations of the everyday. It freed him up to discover passions he did not even know he had, and through this he found out something about himself. In what would later mark a seminal shift in his creative output, he realised he was a poet.

But one cannot become a prodigy overnight. His first poems, shown proudly to his friends, were wordy and lacking in flow. Wiseman said in affectionate chastisement of his childhood friend, referencing a criticism of Meredith likening it 'to a lady who liked to put on all her jewellery after breakfast: don't overdo it'.[3]

Aside from Ronald discovering the poet within, there was to be something else that this Christmas holiday would be remembered for. This was to be the last time that the party would be together. In many ways, this was Bilbo's party with the Dwarves of Erebor writ into reality; a comfortable, joyous feeling of hygge before ardour of active service.

Ronald continued his poetry upon his return to Oxford. He wrote several poems for Edith, including one of the fae folk, explored entirely differently to how he would in Middle-Earth. His verse for Edith, 'Goblin Feet', speaks of 'flittermice' (bats), leprechauns and gnomes, at Edith's request, as she was a self-professed fan of what she called 'little elfin people'. Edith enjoyed the verse, but Tolkien also sent all his poems to G.B. Smith, who was encouraging but still critical. Smith, ever the modernist, tried to convince Tolkien that this might be the perfect opportunity for his friend to expand his reading horizons by trying more modern poets, including the then-topical writings of Rupert Brooke. But Tolkien was resolute in his rejection of the modern, he already had the inkling of where he was to get his inspiration.

Before war broke out, he stumbled upon a series of sentences in his studies, two lines from Cynewulf's *Crist* (a collection of Old English religious poems), '*Eala Earendel engla beorhtast!/ofer middangeard monnum sended*' which fascinated him. The translation of these lines, 'hail Earendel brightest of angels/above the middle-earth sent unto men',[4] is fairly rote for the type of text this was, but the word *Earendel* fascinated Tolkien. His 'Anglo-Saxon Dictionary' (in Tolkien's time the term 'Anglo-Saxon' was the academic standard to describe Old English) defined it as a shining light or ray, but Ronald was convinced in these lines it meant something more. It perhaps did not, in pre-Norman England, Christianity often bestowed celestial significance through rays of light (as a way to bridging the gap between the seen, observable natural phenomena of pagan worship and the unseen, unknowable Christian god), but to Ronald it meant something much more. So much so that, before he declared himself a poet, he penned some lines about it whilst staying at the farm his aunt and brother now kept with the Brookes-Smiths. Many identify this verse, and the rest of the poem, as the origin of what would become Middle-Earth.

But each of the TCBS-ites was to fight in his own private war, alone. First, Gilson went to the Front. Initially, he was hopeful that he should not be fighting in Europe, where the battle was most fierce, but instead in Egypt. His hope was further raised by the order for troops to acquire desert packs. However, those hopes were soon dashed; soon after packs were acquired a new message was sent from the brass: they were headed for Europe after all.

Even before he hit the fight, Rob Gilson was in a turmoil. He was studying Classics at Cambridge, and as such was party to the company of Wiseman, but also Sidney Barrowclough and T.K. 'Teacake' Barnsley, two members of the broader TCBS circle from their schooldays. As they grew up, Wiseman and he grew apart from Barrowclough and Teacake. They were separated by an uncommon humour; Gilson and Wiseman could be playful but the other two seemingly refused to grow up, unable to take anything seriously and positively drowning under layers of their own affected irony. On the eve of war, and in a place of learning, Gilson and Wiseman begun to hate the company of their former friends, and were glad when the Council of London re-centred the TCBS as the four of them and them alone. In its heyday, the TCBS had ballooned out from Gilson, Wiseman and Tolkien's initial friendship group into a collection of at least nine boys: the core four (although G.B. Smith of course joined later), brothers Wilfrid and Ralph Payton ('Whiffy' and 'the Baby', respectively), Sidney Barrowclough, T.K. Barnsley, and the late Vincent Trough. The core four (and Vincent before G.B. Smith) shared deeper passions than snacking in the library and joshing, but the other boys did not. Naturally, as they grew up they drifted apart, still fond of each other (perhaps with the exception of the two Cantabridgean halves, who were stuck in quarters too close to let their hearts grow fonder), but not sharing that brethren bond the core four did.

Even aside from his friendships, Cambridge was not the idyll Rob had hoped for. He was studying Classics but was still an artist at heart, and had turned his professional attention to the edifice. He wanted to be an architect, and so was priming himself for many years of vocational training after graduation, and then to have a war with no definitive end consume even more of his youth was wearing on him.

Although he loved his fellow TCBS-ites, he was also becoming distant from them in his training. He was no longer writing to them, even passing on a collection of Tolkien's poems to Wiseman after a fortnight, unread. Tolkien's own letters to Rob went unanswered for months, and the friends began to worry about what could be vexing their close companion.

In truth, it was nothing the club had done, but affairs of family and the heart. For many years, Rob had become a close friend of an American family called King, through their connection to his headmaster father. He loved and respected them as friends, but recently had also fallen for the young lady of the house, Mr King's daughter, Estelle. When he confessed his feelings to her, she had reacted with shock, and her father had reacted with anger, calling Gilson a man of no prospects and forbidding any kind of betrothal, decreeing he would rather lose Rob as a friend than have him marry his daughter.

So Rob went to train for war thoroughly crushed and heartbroken. No doubt he wanted to tell his fellow TCBS-ites of his plight, but strangely – although they were each other's closest confidants in almost all matters – they operated on a self-imposed silence on matters of the heart and romance. It is unclear why; all four were sensitive men who often spoke of their emotional pains to each other, and were comfortable doing so without feeling the need to feign machismo, and yet somehow all of them felt a great anxiety about discussing their loves with the club. There seemed to be an unspoken feeling that perhaps a lover would turn the men's focus away from the club too much, and they would lose their way.

Nonetheless, although it pained him, Rob kept his silence, until several months passed and he wrote to Tolkien, apologising and expressing admiration for his poems, which he had now read. The chums were whole again, and wrote vociferously to each other once more. For the meanwhile, Rob had overcome his feelings for Estelle, and was content to chat with his friends and sketch. He provided a sketch for G.B. Smith to go with one of his poems, and longed for the group to be reunited in person once more.

Amazingly, Rob got his wish. Through planning and good fortune, the group was reunited one last time at Lichfield, Staffordshire on 25 September 1915. There, thoroughly relieved that there were not many other soldiers billeted here, allowing them to escape from the reality of military life, they spoke of their dreams and wishes, and Rob sketched the nearby cathedral.

Perhaps this final council with his friends gave him the clarity of heart and mind he sorely needed, for before he would be posted to active service (and he was the first of the four-square TCBS to go) he was able to finally settle things with Estelle.

This is a debt he owes greatly to his stepmother, Marianne 'Donna' Gilson, who although she could never replace the mother he lost, did love him as her own child and knew his heart, sometimes better than he did.

Upon finding out about the unpleasant business with Estelle King, Donna would stop at nothing until she could find a way to get Estelle and Rob to meet once more, away from the King patriarch. And she succeeded, and Rob poured out his heart to Estelle, and Estelle poured out hers to him. It turned out that, although she had indeed been shocked by his proposal, she did not share her father's feelings about him, and was quite in love with him too. They talked it out, and agreed to be married, though kept the engagement secret for now (though of course Donna knew), so as to avoid the wrath of Estelle's father.

And so Rob went to war a changed man; feeling no longer crushed by his circumstances but emboldened by his future with his fiancée and his friends, determined to make it out to return to her. He now wrote vociferously once more, to both the TCBS and Estelle (and though Estelle heard plenty of his TCBS friends, it pained his heart that – due to their secret engagement – he could not do the same the other way round).

Estelle herself was no passive party in the war effort. In spite of her wealthy American family meaning that she had no need to join the war, she was motivated to help as best she could, and so joined the volunteer nurses several weeks after Rob was posted.

And now to the next to be taken as an active party: Geoffrey Bache Smith. G.B.S. had now thrown himself into his poetry as much as an outlet for his frustration with the army as out of a desire to create *something* before he saw active duty, lest he not return home. He, like Tolkien, was a sensitive spirit, ill-suited for fighting, but unlike Tolkien he did not have that streak of 'outdoorsiness' that helped Ronald through some of the mundanities of trench warfare and training that were nightmarish for G.B. Smith. His letters intoned his grim mood, and frustration with the whole thing almost to the point of comic absurdity, disliking the militarism of the military he had volunteered to serve. Nonetheless, as he was the first of the Oxford duo to go into training, he at least could act as a literal field guide for Ronald, which he did with aplomb, advising him on what to pack and what not to pack. Although with the benefit of hindsight of a modern audience his advice such as not to bring a table and chair (he planned to buy a soap box for both) and to pack some writing and painting equipment, for there was more waiting around than he'd expected, may seem by turns obvious or frivolous, it indicates just how many people from Tolkien and Smith's social strata were woefully unprepared for the war they enthusiastically joined at the behest of Lord Kitchener.

Although there was some social variation within the TCBS (Tolkien being lower middle class and Gilson being upper middle class) they were all still of the middle class, and therefore, due to the absurdity of the class system of Britain, were billeted to officer roles automatically, as the working class were foot soldiers, and the upper class were highest ranking officers. It seems absurd to organise a military not on expertise or experience, but on socio-economic status, but by the 1900s British war efforts were absurd. Psychologically, the nationalist pride from the era of the Victorian Empire clouded sense. Britain saw itself as indefatigable in the face of huge, and in hindsight, obvious threats. War was, to the minds of the British public, a noble and patriotic pursuit, a chance for glory, as opposed to the horrifying human cost paid for the failure of diplomacy.

And so foot soldiers were led by people who had be told not to bring a table and chair with them to the trenches. The naiveté with which so many middle class folk joined up cost them dearly. On average, one in eight British soldiers who went to war never came back. In the middle classes, that number was one in five. Whole friendship groups were encouraged to sign up, as if they could recapture the abstract prideful whimsy of Sparta, where warrior friends and lovers fought side-by-side. John Garth excellently captures this mindset, writing of how, to middle-class men of Tolkien's generation, war was this great and grand thing of antiquity and Greek verses, more akin to a sport than a nightmare.[5]

At this time, G.B. Smith seemed to fall somewhere between the jingoistic narrow patriotism he had been fed at school and the sobering reality of war which he was about to experience. On the one hand, he was prone to dramatic exclamations and crusading rhetoric. In that same vein, he was an avowed fan of Rupert Brooke, whose poetry captures the naive romantic patriotism of the early middle-class war effort, and who died before he could see the reality of trench warfare, and read the evocative and real *Dolce et Decorum est* by Wilfred Owen. However, G.B.S. also had something of Owen's contemporary and friend Siegfried Sassoon in him, for his letters to the rest of the TCBS, and Tolkien especially, rung with a clear fear and fatalism. He often wrote of whether or not he would come back, what he would be happy for if he died the next day, and so on, but these were not romantic abstract fancies, but very real fears. Now posted out with the 19th Battalion of the Lancashire Fusiliers, he could see and feel the difference between who was suited for war and who wasn't, as well as the harsh realities of the war itself. The former TCBS-ite T.K. 'Teacake' Barnsley seemed to be thriving, having now given up his previous dream of being a Christian minister to dedicate himself to the life of a career soldier. Tolkien and G.B.S. marvelled at the difference between themselves and their former school chum. Mechanised death and poison clouds on a grand scale were a far cry from 'noble' warfare with sabres, which both G.B.S. and Tolkien had been trained in the use of. Both men would see gas attacks, tanks, countless war-wounded succumb to their injuries or infection, and the Germans use flamethrowers to decimate the British and French troops.[6] Additionally, G.B.S. knew himself to be ill-suited for war on a fundamental level. He was exhausted and unable to sleep and lost weight through army training as opposed to gaining muscle. He saw his peers and privates react faster and deal better with the challenges and stresses of war, and saw many like him killed, that – as if almost gifted with foresight – he poured much of his efforts into encouraging Tolkien to do what he was unlikely to be able to: to tell his story to the world, to publish, and invite others into this fantasy kingdom that brought G.B.S. so much joy in his darkest hours.

Wiseman was the final one of Tolkien's friends to join up. He was the only one of the core TCBS four not to have graduated with a grade equivalent higher than a second class, and felt ashamed of this. However, his mathematics degree was not to be sniffed at: in 1915 he saw a recruitment advertisement for the Royal Navy. They sought mathematicians to train to become on-board instructors, so he wrote to Tolkien on 11 July of that year. He was headed to Greenwich for his training in both his military role and the basics of life at sea.

On 2 January 1916, he reported for duty in Invergordon, Scotland, to serve aboard HMS *Superb* as a naval officer. He wrote to Tolkien, expressing his nervousness about being aboard with hundreds of men he did not know, and who didn't know him.[7] This must have only been compounded by the time at which he joined the battleship, for it was berthed in Cromarty Firth, where an armoured cruiser had exploded without known cause, costing the lives of 300 men aboard, and ratcheting up fear and suspicion that German submarines were hunting the Firth fleet. To combat this, the *Superb* and other large battleships were berthed surrounded by 40ft of torpedo nets on all sides. Wiseman (and all others

The 1892 Tolkien Family Christmas card sent from Bloemfontein to their family in England. From left to right: Arthur Tolkien, a housemaid (name unknown), Mabel Tolkien (seated), Isaak, a nursemaid (name unknown), and baby John Ronald Reuel Tolkien. (*Public domain*)

The Tolkien boys (John Ronald on the left and Hilary on the right) circa 1905. (*Public domain*)

Sarehole Mill in Birmingham, where Tolkien spent the most formative years of his childhood. (*Tanya Dedyukhina*)

Mabel Tolkien's grave at St Peter's Catholic Church, Bromsgrove. It is fitted with a cross similar to those of the Oratory Fathers. (*Gentry Graves*)

Photograph of Mr Measures' House at King Edward's School, circa 1911. Robert Quilter Gilson is the boy on the farthest left of the second row from the bottom, Ronald Tolkien is seated next to Mr Measures on the left, and Christopher Wiseman is seated farthest on the right. (*The King Edward's Foundation archive*)

Tolkien's aunt Jane Neave, circa 1900, aged 28. (*Public domain*)

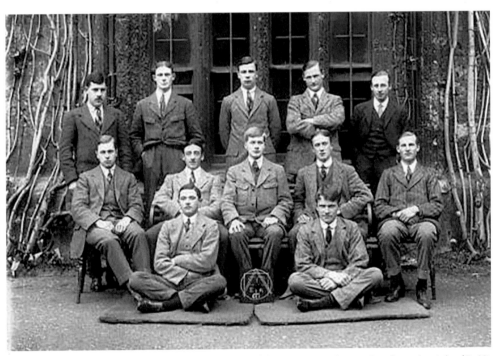

The Aplousticks, the club Tolkien founded at Oxford. Tolkien is seated second in from the right. (*Public domain*)

Tolkien circa 1911, aged 19.
(*Public domain*)

Tolkien in 1916, during his time as a
second lieutenant of the Lancashire
Fusiliers in the First World War, aged 24.
(*Public domain*)

The Tolkiens' first house in Northmoor Road, Oxford: number 22. (*Stefan Servos*)

Number 20 Northmoor Road. The Tolkiens lived here from 1930-47, and the building now bears a blue plaque. (*Jonathan P Bowen*)

The first page of the Beowulf manuscript in Cotton Vitellius A. xv. Tolkien's scholarship elevated Beowulf to a major text within the English canon. (*Image is provided by the British Library, under public domain. Alteration (cropping) Earthsound*)

The words 'Tengwar' (an Elven script Tolkien created), 'Sindarin' (an Elven language Tolkien created), and 'Quenya' (a more ancient Elven language Tolkien created) in Tengwar script. Tolkien's invented languages are so dense and complex that scholars still study them to this day. (*Olaf Studt, font credit 'Tengwar Formal' by Michal 'miszka' Nowakowski*)

Tolkien in 1931 (aged 39). (*Elliott and Fry*)

The White Tree of Gondor, one of the
iconic symbols Tolkien created for his world.
(*Nabitbitcom*)

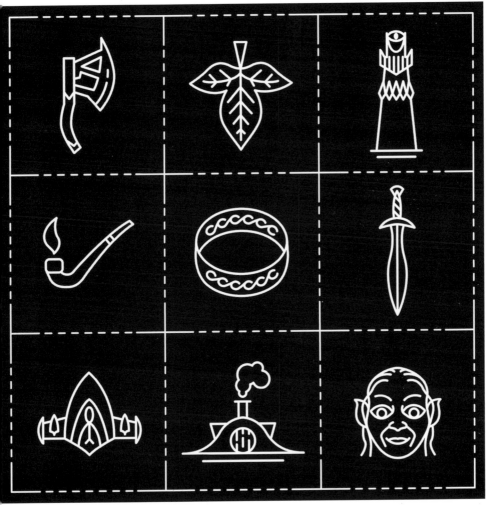

Artist Antikwar's abstracted renditions of nine images from the Tolkien mythos. Middle-Earth's popularity is so vast that elements of its mythos can be recognised in almost any art style. (*Antikwar*)

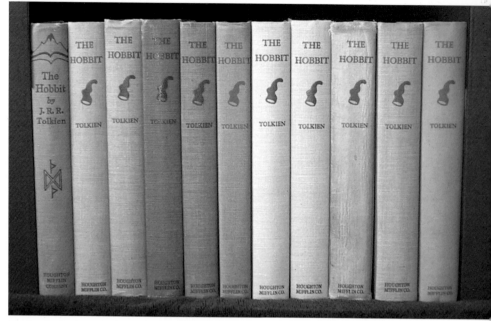

Twelve 2nd editions of *The Hobbit*, published by Houghton Mifflin Company in the USA. Houghton Mifflin had to race to catch up to the demand for Tolkien books in the 1960s, which was initially filled by pirate versions. (*Strebe*)

A painting of Tolkien as he appeared in the 1980s. (*Anna Tochennikova*)

Edith and Ronald Tolkien's grave, bearing the inscription Beren for him and Lúthien for her, in honour of the fact that their romance inspired that story in his legendarium. (*MNStudio*)

A collection of Middle-Earth works by J.R.R. Tolkien, published by HarperCollins. Although he spent most of his life writing stories set in Middle-Earth, aside from *The Hobbit* and *The Lord of the Rings*, all of Tolkien's other Middle-Earth works were published posthumously. (Eeli Purola)

Faith Tolkien's bust of her father-in-law J.R.R. Tolkien, standing in his alma mater Exeter College, Oxford. (*James Jensen*)

Fully adopted into British mythlore: a 2004 UK postage stamp showing part of Tolkien's map of Middle-Earth. (*PictureLake*)

JRR TOLKIEN · THE LORD OF THE RINGS

Priscilla Tolkien, circa 2005. Tolkien's youngest child and only daughter, she serves as Honorary Vice-President of the Tolkien Society, one of the plaintiffs who sued Warner Bros for improper use of the Middle-Earth licence. (*Sancho Proudfoot*)

Part of the set of the Shire for *The Hobbit* films in Matamata, New Zealand. Tolkien's memory of his childhood home in Sarehole inspired the Shire's rustic, pre-Industrial aesthetic. (*Anupam Hatui*)

who wished to board), had to climb 40ft of rope ladder over the torpedo net to enter the ship.

Less than a week later, Gilson had been promoted to second lieutenant, and sailed to France to serve (on the same day Estelle King boarded the ship that would take her to Holland to nurse the war-wounded). Serving in France, the presence of death and devastation in the wake of the battles made him tremendously depressed. He was a sensitive young man, who was acquainted with grief and loss thanks to the early death of his mother, and friend Vincent, and he took comfort in art and architecture: legacy and edifice that could outlast the people who built them. Here the things that he used to cope with grief were destroyed by the very same forces. His letters out took on a resigned and melancholy tone. The effort taken by each side to hide from the shells of the other deeply disturbed him. When he got his first taste of trench warfare in No Man's Land on 2 February, he suffered a hallucination. Of his dreamy younger, undergraduate self, meeting himself now, crawling on his belly through mud on a winter's night in no man's land. It was so surreal he had to fight to suppress his laughter at the idea.[8]

On 1 July 1916, Rob Gilson's father, still the King Edward's headmaster, was hosting the school sports day. Although he was usually accompanied by his wife to hand out prizes, this year she had given it a miss to rest at home. Rob's sister Molly was there, though, serving tea for the boys' parents. Hundreds of miles away, Rob was waving his men over the top, and leading them into what would become an infamous British military disaster. The Somme offensive at Albert was already being discussed in papers back home before it had happened. Rob was tasked with commanding his men into no man's land that morning, expecting that the German troops had been 'cleared' before by a shell barrage. But they had not. They waited until the British had started making inroads into no man's land before returning fire, filling the air with vast artillery shells. Gilson and his men were commanded over after the Germans had started shelling no man's land. They made it over the top, and Rob, who had dreaded commanding and leading other men in the trenches, faced his fear admirably. He kept advancing, leading his men forwards 'calmly and courageously' according to the eyewitness report of his injured captain.[9]

But bravery was not enough. Rob Gilson and his batmen were hit with an artillery shell. Both men died, though it is unclear if it was instant or not, and some of the surviving men described Rob's body as looking as if it had been dragged, or had dragged itself, to the trenches, but it was too late. By the time he was found, he was long dead.

Naturally, this news shook the TCBS. G.B. Smith urged unity amongst the survivors, but Tolkien sank into his darker thoughts, declaring them no longer whole and therefore that the TCBS was over.[10] After a flurry of correspondence between Wiseman, Smith and Tolkien, Tolkien relented, and the surviving TCBS-ites decided that, although they truly were no longer whole, they were also still the TCBS, always and forever, and they made even more of an effort to be there for each other for the rest of their lives, no matter how long or short that would be.

It would be impossible to say who felt Gilson's death most keenly out of his surviving friends, for they all felt it so differently. Tolkien sank into a deep melancholia. Wiseman was racked with survivor's guilt, that his time aboard the *Superb* was so relatively easy in comparison to what his friends were enduring, and what had killed Rob. And G.B. Smith, the poet, extolled heavy letters and verse on the subject of death and loss with a new-found fatalism.

It seemed as if Smith truly did not believe that he could survive the war. Once, upon receiving the latest of Tolkien's verses he praised it, emphasising that if he died later that day he would be happy because he died after having read it. Smith and Tolkien, the geographically closest of the surviving TCBS-ites during this phase of the war, were able to visit each other a few times. This support was no doubt immeasurably helpful to both men after the passing of their mutual friend, giving Smith someone to vent his feelings to and Tolkien someone whose presence filled him with a bright joy to burn through his darker thoughts.

But alas, it was not to last. On 29 November, Smith, who was eagerly awaiting some upcoming leave, was supervising some road repairs. A rogue German howitzer shell exploded next to him in the road, injuring his buttock and arm with the shrapnel. If anything, he considered himself lucky: nothing vital was injured. He walked to the dressing station under his own power. He smoked a cigarette whilst waiting for an ambulance to take him to the casualty clearing station, and wrote to his mother, assuring her that he was fine, and not to worry, in spite of news of his injury. Once inside the clearing station he relaxed further: he was familiar with and on friendly terms with several of the nurses managing his care.[11]

However, after two days, disaster struck. It became clear that Geoffrey had contracted gas gangrene, a pernicious disease contracted from infected trench soil entering wounds. It got its name from the most fatal symptom: the infection necrotises living tissue, the process of which fills it with gas. The wound on Smith's buttock was the source of the infection, which quickly spread to his thigh. He endured an operation to remove the infected tissue, but it was too late. His body was overwhelmed by the infection, and G.B. Smith passed away 3 December 1916, leaving behind a distraught mother, whose prior correspondence with him had been a dictated letter assuring her that he was in no danger.

This loss was devastating to all who knew G.B. Smith. Wiseman still felt useless and powerless, a world away in his floating island as his friends perished one by one. Worse still, he had to break the news to Tolkien of Geoffrey's death.[12] And Tolkien never fully recovered. The combined loss of Rob and Geoffrey changed him, and was something he carried with him for the rest of his days. These friends had been his creative lights; he sketched inspired by Rob's art, and wrote under the admiration and critique of fellow poet Geoffrey. He mourned G.B. Smith's unfinished poem, *The Burial of Sophocles*, and Gilson's unfulfilled engagement to Estelle King, whom he had never even got to meet in Rob's lifetime. And, of course, he mourned the loss of two of his closest companions. With them gone, it could be argued that now the only people with whom he had shared even his more secret side, and therefore the only people who truly knew him, were Edith and Christopher. Everyone else had perished.

Chapter 9

Remembrance

There is something about death in Middle-Earth that speaks directly to Tolkien's four months of active combat in World War I. It does not have the sanitised remoteness of death in myth, it is direct, ugly, random, and painful. Battles in Middle-Earth may be epic in scale, but they do not feel epic in a positive sense; they feel nightmarish, overwhelming and frightening. The sense of fatality that the main characters have, usually hobbits, unaccustomed to fighting, is palpable. And yet they do not flee.

No hobbits are pressured into active service as Tolkien and his friends were, but there is still no sense of desire for battle-glory. Bilbo is swept up in a gruesome dispute between two refugee populations, fanned by Elven interests and interrupted by the forces of a grieving son seeking vengeance. Frodo and Sam are tossed this way and that over Middle-Earth by the Orcs who captured them, and Merry and Pippin end up fighting alongside communities they had scarcely even heard of prior to their quest.

'One War is enough for any man.'[1] So wrote Tolkien to his son Michael in 1940, after he followed in his father's footsteps by volunteering for service in active conflict. However, Michael, an officer cadet at Sandhurst at the time of his father's letter, was far more suited to military life than his father, by Tolkien's own proud admission.

Not that being suited for the military was necessarily enough to save you, as Ronald knew all too well by the end of his brief time in the military. The boisterous former TCBS-ite T.K. 'Tea Cake' Barnsley seemed to be flourishing on the battlefield, and had become a captain. In August of 1916, T.K. was completely buried alive by a trench mortar, though he miraculously survived, and returned to England to recover in a military hospital before entering back into the fray. However, almost exactly a year after his brush with death, his luck ran out. In August 1917, he was stationed near Ypres, and stopped to console a captured prisoner of war. This moment of pause cost him his life, and he was killed in action.

Barnsley was not the only member of the wider TCBS lost: Ralph Payton, nicknamed 'the Baby' at school due to being the younger of the two Payton brothers who were members of the TCBS, joined up early during his time at the University of Cambridge, much like T.K., serving in the same battalion as him (the 1st Birmingham). He fell before his friend, killed in action on 22 July 1916. His name is inscribed on Thiepval Memorial, but his body was never identified. He was survived by his older brother, Wilfrid Payton, another member of Tolkien's broader schoolboy friendship circle. By the end of the war, five of the nine members of the broader TCBS were dead; four of them felled during the Great War.

But what of Ronald? His military career started on 15 July 1915, and was hardly illustrious in spite of the huge personal toll it took on the young scholar. He did fight in the Battle of the Somme, but was invalided off the battlefield more than once, emaciated by sickness and hard labour, eventually spending most of his active service as an officer requisitioned to garrison duties. This started when he contracted trench fever from lice during the Battle of the Somme. A second lieutenant in the Lancashire Fusiliers, Tolkien struggled in the military, a far cry from the treasured childhood memory of his cadet days in St Philip's Officers' Training Corps, lining the road on George V's coronation. Unmitigated pressure, desperate conditions, and a woeful lack of understanding of the psychological toll of modern warfare, meant that Tolkien was entering the British Army at its most relentless. Writing at the time, Ronald confided to Edith (now his wife) that 'Gentlemen are rare among the superiors, and even human beings rare indeed.'[2] His situation worsened when, on 2 June 1916, Tolkien received a telegram to scramble to Folkestone for deployment to France.

Yet even before he joined the army, Ronald's life was disrupted, and his precarious social position threatened once again. 'In those days chaps joined up, or were scorned publicly. It was a nasty cleft to be in for a young man with too much imagination and little physical courage,'[3] he told Michael. Tolkien was barely able to delay service until he had finished his degree, and enlisted just after his finals, as his relatives (frustrated by his iconoclastic engagement and reluctance to join the war effort) had pressured him to.[4]

After having fought so hard for Edith's hand in marriage, going against the will of his dear guardian Fr. Morgan, Edith's family, and of course the family of her previous fiancé, the young couple's vows were taken under a grim pall. War was consuming their generation, as he recalled to Michael 'Think of your mother! [...] I was a young fellow, with a moderate degree, [...] a few dwindling pounds [...] and no prospects, [...] in the infantry where the chances of survival were against you heavily.'[5] Although Ronald and Edith were lucky enough to survive, the fact that half of the Tea Club and Barrovian Society – the friends that inspired Tolkien's lifelong dedication to poetry – had not, had weighed on him ever since.

Ronald's own experience of the army was clouded by death. There was the death of Rob, of Geoffrey, of Thomas (TK) and Ralph. There was the inability to mourn any of them fully and the correspondence with his surviving closest friends eventually dwindled to just Christopher Wiseman (who was dealing with his own guilt on-board the *Superb*, whilst also providing mathematical and navigational expertise that saved the ship more than once). There were the mundanities of the tasks after the deaths: collating all Geoffrey's poems to send to his mother at her request; passing on his condolences to his old school master for the death of his son; his old friend for the death of his younger brother.

Tolkien was made a signals officer of the 11th Service Battalion of the Fusiliers on 7 June 1916 and put in command of the enlisted men. He chafed against his role as their leader, the military protocol prohibiting friendship between 'other ranks', and against the leadership structure of the army as a whole, finding, 'The most improper job of any man [...] is bossing other men. Not one in a million is fit for it, and least of all those who seek the opportunity.'[6] Most of the men under Tolkien's charge did not survive the war; his battalion was almost completely wiped out during the Somme, Tolkien himself only escaping the same fate due to being invalided to England. But being able to mix with working-class men outside of academia, or the sprawling industrial heart of Edgbaston, Tolkien developed what he would later call a 'deep sympathy and feeling for the "Tommy", especially the plain soldier from the agricultural counties'.[7]

This sympathy for the 'Tommy' was the inspiration for one of Tolkien's most beloved characters: Frodo's gardener and loyal companion, Samwise Gamgee. Sam represents the honesty, loyalty, kind-heartedness and stalwart character Tolkien recognised in the men under his command. However, unlike him, Sam and Frodo are able to develop a friendship that transcends their class boundary. Although Frodo initially needs a push to see Sam as someone who is not his servant whilst they are on their quest, the friendship that blossoms between them is one of equals, where they both learn from and teach each other new things. This is perhaps a small amount of wish fulfilment on Tolkien's part, for another of the army's rules which he loathed but was forced to comply to was a strict enforcement of class structure: meaning that friendships between middle-class officers and working-class soldiers were strictly prohibited. Tolkien wanted very much to talk to his men and enjoy their company, especially one young soldier whom he overheard seemingly creating his own language in the mess hall but it was not to be.[8] And so, feeling alienated by fellow officers, forbidden from fraternising with his men, and with a steadily dwindling pool of close friends to confide in by letter, Tolkien's war was a lonely one.

Outside of coded letters to Edith (telling her roughly where he was in France whilst avoiding the British Army's postal censorship) and the fatherly advice he bestowed upon Michael years later, Ronald spoke little of his time in the army, though the long shadow of the lost lives of his men and friends manifested in his work. Writing in 1960 to Professor L. W. Forster he specified that – though he pushed against direct allegorical readings of his work – the Great War certainly influenced the 'landscape' of Middle-Earth. Perhaps the most telling statement Tolkien ever made on his time in combat was that the Dead Marshes of Middle-Earth 'owe something to Northern France after the Battle of the Somme'.[9] The Dead Marshes, created by fields churned in bloody conflict, where visions of the corpses of the fallen can still be seen centuries later just under the foetid water's surface, are a far less sanitised form of remembrance than the poppies of our world. Tolkien started the manuscript that would become *The Lord of the Rings* over a decade later, but the staunch anti-war narrative of every tale in that world speaks of a creative mind scarred by enduring a devastating conflict decades before. Although good always triumphs over evil in Middle-Earth, it is with sacrifice; the heavy weight of death and despair is acknowledged and grieved through the losses of Thorin, Boromir, Théoden, etc. Frodo – melancholy and traumatised by his quest – speaks not with the bombast of Rupert Brooke but the world-weary pain of Wilfred Owen.

That said, Tolkien was loath to have his work claimed as war literature, least of all for the Second World War. He was contacted by many fans who wondered if *The Lord of the Rings* was allegorical, in whole or in part, to the Second World War. This became a source of great frustration for Tolkien, forcing him to take up his pen to clarify in the preface to the 2nd Edition of *The Lord of the Rings*.

'One has indeed personally to come under the shadow of war to feel fully its oppression; but as the years go by it seems now often forgotten that to be caught in youth by 1914 was no less hideous an experience than to be involved in 1939 and the following years. By 1918 all but one of my close friends were dead.'[10]

To Ronald, it seemed that the memory of what was meant to be the 'war to end all wars' was already fading, but for the rest of his life, its impact was not something he could shed.

Chapter 10

Oxford, Leeds and Back Again

Invalided away back to England, in many ways, Tolkien was one of the lucky ones. He still had much of his health, he survived, and perhaps at some point he could return to starting that illustrious career that First Class Degree offered him, but of course he did not feel lucky. For one thing, mental health was so poorly understood, and the depression he had learned to live with for so long surely dampened his symptoms, but given how he reacted to certain stresses, and what came through in his writing, it seems likely that he suffered from 'shell-shock', or post-traumatic stress disorder as we'd call it today. And, in some ways, he would miss the loss of Rob and Geoffrey for the rest of his life. But he would not let their ideals and their inspirations die with them. He drew vociferously for the rest of his days, shadowing his painter friend, and as for Geoffrey… his letters of encouragement about the poetry Tolkien wrote set in his private fantasy world stirred something in him. He now felt that whatever this story (stories? A mythos?) was inside him it had the potential to be something great, and so, to honour his fallen friend, he endeavoured to carry out his wish. And so he got to work with fervour. What had been mere shadows of Middle-Earth until now started to grow into something that Ronald couldn't yet comprehend. His only surviving childhood friend, Christopher Wiseman, urged him on in kind, 'Start the epic.'[1]

Of course, Tolkien had other reasons for creating Middle-Earth, and other ways of keeping G.B. Smith's memory alive. Together with G.B. Smith's mother (Ruth) and Christopher, they collated his poems, publishing them posthumously in the collection *A Spring Harvest*. He also kept in written correspondence with Ruth for the rest of her life. There is perhaps a tragic echo to their circumstances: that a man who lost his mother when he was just a boy and a woman who lost her son long before his time should form such a friendship. And his other motivation for creating the body of work that would become Middle-Earth was fantastical, bold and (by his own admission in adage) overconfident and arrogant. He sought to create a mythology for England, something akin to the *Kalevala* of Finland, which he held in such high regard.

Although there were other works of Tolkien's that found their way into Middle-Earth canon (for example, *The Man In the Moon Fell Down Too Soon*, a contemporary piece to *Goblin Feet*, was eventually serialised in *The Adventures of Tom Bombadil*. It is also given prominence in Peter Jackson's extended edition of *The Hobbit: An Unexpected Journey*, when Bofur the Dwarf sings it at Rivendell), it was at this time that Tolkien penned the first set of stories with an idea towards putting together a unified fantasy canon. Tolkien's first attempt was heavily inspired by Morris' *An Earthly Paradise*, for it tells of a voyager called Eriol who washes up on a strange land and hears tall tales from the local folk.

Outside of the world inside his head, war was still raging. Racked with survivor's guilt, Tolkien was torn between wanting to continue his writing to honour his friend, his sense of duty to return, and his intense fear of returning only to die. He was under no illusions about his role in war, or rather, how against his nature war was. He was a timid, gentle sort, entirely unsuited and undesiring of battle-glory and the violent trench warfare he had been flung into by circumstance. It is clear to see that writing about war from this perspective was something that he did for the rest of his life: writing as Bilbo for *The Hobbit* and his nephew Frodo in *The Lord of the Rings*. Both hobbits are thrust into a world outside of their understanding against their will. Unlike many myths and fantasy stories, battles are not sanitised in Tolkien's writing; it is bloody, and awful, and uncertain, and frightening. And perhaps crucially, it is something that the heroes are allowed to be frightened of. Bravery isn't the lack of acknowledgement of fear in Tolkien's world, nor is it bloodthirsty or vengeful. Courage is often simply surviving as best you can.

He was extremely fortunate that his health kept him away from the front line for the rest of the war. His fevers would not subside, and when they did they would flare up again. Not to mention, the possibly that he had PTSD was very real; it is entirely possible that even the thought of going back to the trenches, after having seen what he'd seen, and losing who he'd lost, was making him sick again. At one point he was well enough to try to pass an examination to make him signals officer of the Yorkshire camp, a post that would have kept him in Britain, but he failed the exam, then fell ill again, this time being transferred to Brooklands Officers' Hospital in Hull. This was a place he found infinitely more soothing; a friend from the Lancashire Fusiliers was there, and he struck up what was to become a lifelong friendship with a visiting nun.

Edith and Jennie visited when they could, which was not often, travelling from the cramped dampness of their boarding house room in Hornsea. They were miserable there, and Edith – now heavily pregnant – was determined that she and the baby would not have to welcome it there. So they moved back to Cheltenham, which was still Edith's heart-home, boarding until the baby was born. Whilst Edith prepared to give birth to her first child, Ronald was desperate to be with her, but was completely bedridden. To keep his mind occupied, he created something all his own, a tale of a character called Turin, and the touchstone for what would eventually become *The Children of Hurin*.

Baby John Francis Reuel Tolkien (named for his grandfathers and Father Francis) was born in Cheltenham on 16 November 1917, after a long and difficult labour, in which Edith had nearly died, and a recovery period which she had to undergo alone. Ronald had been discharged, but now he was serving at the camp, and try as he might he could not get leave granted. When he eventually got to see Edith and the baby for the first time, John was already a week old. But it was still a joyous occasion; Father Francis travelled from Birmingham to baptise the boy, and Edith, Jennie and the baby moved to rooms in Roos, Yorkshire. Ronald had just been promoted to full lieutenant, and so was likely to be staying in Britain at the camp for the foreseeable future, much to Edith's and his own relief.

This was a happy time for the couple. New parents, with a new-found sense of safety after the turmoil of Ronald being on the front lines, his faltering health and Edith's traumatic pregnancy. Both of them felt renewed, and would often walk in the woods together, talking as they had when they were sweethearts. One day when they were walking together, they stumbled across a hemlock grove, which they both found deeply beautiful. Edith, inspired by the sight, began to sing and dance for Ronald, which he found deeply moving.

This was to inspire the centrepiece story of *The Silmarillion* (and Tolkien's favourite of his own works): the tale of Beren and Lúthien. Beren is a mortal man who falls for Lúthien, an immortal elf woman who Beren first meets when she is dancing and singing through a hemlock grove. Although there are many echoes of Edith in how Tolkien writes women, Lúthien was the only one that Ronald actively identified with her. Lúthien is a wise and loving elf maid, who – together with Beren – rescues one of the silmarils from Melkor's own crown. It is touching to see that Ronald identified himself and Edith as a unit that – when together – could defeat unstoppable odds. However, once again, the fetishisation of grieving women blights Lúthien as a character. As an elf in love with a mortal, Lúthien is fated to waste away into grief after Beren's death, much as Arwen is after Aragorn's, millennia later. That Elven-human love comes with such a heavy toll of grief, not only the denial of their mortality, but also an excruciating and long life after, and that these relationships are only ever explored with a female elf and a male human, once again speaks to this deifying of female pain in Tolkien's work.

Nonetheless, Beren and Lúthien is Tolkien's most emotionally ambitious work of that period; the inner worlds of Beren and Lúthien are explored, as is a sweeping epic taking place over decades. Unusually for Tolkien, it is also openly romantic, an epic with a love story at its heart. Tolkien's work usually keeps romance at a distance or off to one side, in favour of focusing on the love of friendship, but in Beren and Lúthien it is centred.

After he had penned this romantic epic, his own love life took a turn for the worse. He was posted to Penkridge, Staffordshire in 1918, and Edith, Jennie and the baby travelled with him as had become their custom, but Edith was growing weary of this life. That is not to say that she or he had wished he return to the war, far from it; just after his move his entire battalion was wiped out: in Chemin des Dames they were all either killed or taken prisoner, causing the battalion to be disbanded on 12 August 1918.

Understandably, this left the Tolkiens shaken but relieved that Ronald had avoided such a fate. However, this of course meant the plans for the soldiers serving on home turf had also changed, and now Ronald was posted back up north scarcely after he and his family had made a home down south. This time, Edith refused to go with him. Taking care of her newborn son was exhausting her, not least because the difficult birth had left her with chronic pain and other lasting health problems. The chaos surrounding the Penkridge posting had to be her line in the sand. And so, Ronald travelled back to the Humber Garrison alone. Although he had been used to this separate life from Edith, being away from her whilst he was still processing the fate of his battalion cost him dear, and he was taken ill once again. Edith joked in a letter to him at the time, 'I should think you ought never to feel tired again, for the amount of Bed [sic] you have had since you came back from France nearly two years ago is enormous.'[2]

Although not written with any malice, this was emblematic of the psyche at the time with regards to the war-wounded whose injuries were not visible. 'Shell-shock', as post-traumatic stress disorder was called then, was only just being described, and England had a poor understanding of mental health and how warfare affects the mind. Out in the trenches, deserters were shot on sight, as the old notions of bravery and cowardice were still in place where empathy and understanding of trauma were sorely needed. For soldiers like Ronald, whose health was impacted from what seems highly likely to be an underlying psychological cause (his PTSD), things were slightly better, he was known to be physically sick, and so his symptoms could be respected and addressed if not the root cause. However, that underlying misunderstanding that still pervaded national consciousness, that only 'weak-willed' men show their trauma from the hellish war, and that courage was putting on a brave face and repressing emotions, meant that many family members and friends would become frustrated with those who fought upon their return, not realising that a certain part of them would never come back.

In the hospital, Tolkien once more passed his time, and more importantly took solace in the mythos he was creating. He continued to work on his stories, poetry and Elven languages, but also took up some real-world languages, teaching himself some basic Russian, and revisiting Spanish and Italian.

When he was finally discharged in October, things were looking up. Peace seemed on the horizon, and so Ronald took this opportunity to go to Oxford and enquire about job opportunities. He arrived, only to discover the university to be a shell of its former self: barely keeping its doors open with its shadow of undrafted staff and a handful of students. This no doubt alarmed him just on its own, but then of course there was the fact that that meant that academic jobs were incredibly scarce. He leaned on all the contacts he possibly could during his brief visit, and drew a blank, until he came to William Craigie. Craigie had been his Icelandic teacher, and as such knew of his linguistic aptitude and broad philological base. This emboldened him to proffer what may have been the perfect job for Tolkien at the time. Craigie was part of the team working on the New English Dictionary, specifically the latter half, and wondered if Tolkien would like to join him in this endeavour as an assistant lexicographer. Naturally, Tolkien jumped at the opportunity, and, when peace was declared on 11 November 1918, he contacted his command to ask if he may stay in Oxford until demobilisation. The reason given officially was completion of his education. He was granted permission, and so by the end of the month he, Edith, Jennie and the baby were safely ensconced in their new home in Oxford. They were finally able to enjoy 'our home together', as Ronald wrote, for this was indeed the first time the couple had lived under the same roof since Father Francis had forced them apart over a decade ago.

In the new year Tolkien began a diary, first in English and then in classical Tolkien style, in an alphabet he was just inventing. This would go on to become the Alphabet of Rumil, an Elven scholar of Middle-Earth. The only problem was that Rumil probably did not record a diary in his alphabet before it was set, but in our world, Tolkien did – and so found the early entries impossible to decipher after a while as he changed the meaning of the characters as he went!

He was greatly enjoying his life as an assistant lexicographer, beavering away with the rest of the small team in the Old Ashmolean. The New English Dictionary was to be the most comprehensive dictionary of English to date at the time. It had been started in 1878, the first two volumes had already been published, but U-Z were unfinished. The project had been ongoing for so long (and further prolonged of course by the war) that the original editor had died in 1915.

Tolkien was to work on the letter W. It was etymologically demanding work in a way he had not experienced before. For example, his definition of the word 'wasp' contained etymological comparisons and traces to thirteen other languages! However, this was exactly the type of work he loved: going on learning tangents and getting deeply immersed in the shape and form of languages. Looking back on his time with the dictionary he said that he 'learned more in those two years than in any other equal period of [his] life'.[3] His boss and editor Dr Henry Bradley was delighted with his work too, enthusiastically singing his praises for a knowledge of Old English and the Germanic languages second to none for one his age.[4]

There was only one problem with working on the dictionary: the hours were so lenient that he and most of the rest of the team were required to make a second income, and most did this through the tutoring of the university students. Tolkien was no exception, and in fact found himself an unusual niche in the teaching market. Lady Margaret Hall and St Hughes were all-women colleges in desperate need of tutors, as custom dictated that all female students needed a chaperone if they were to study with an unwed male tutor. As a married man, Tolkien was a convenient and safe option for female students. Hopefully this duty of educating the next generation of female scholars warmed his heart, as his dearly departed friend Rob Gilson was an avowed feminist.

His tutoring business was so successful that after two years he no longer needed to work at the dictionary. He got on well with his students too; some of them would become lifelong friends not just of him but of the family. This was good for Edith, for she was finding the Oxfordian social strata difficult to navigate. There were many wives for Edith to call on and to call on her, as was expected, but she struggled to fit in there. Unlike her Cheltenham friends, there was not an intermingling of classes, here the social hierarchy was tied to both class and academia, a world which was totally foreign to her. She felt self-conscious and out-of-her-depth, terrified of breaking unknown social rules. For example, when they first moved into a full house in Oxford, as opposed to rented rooms, a few academic wives called on her, leaving two calling cards in a bowl in her entrance hall. The implication was that she would have to visit them in turn to return the second card (perhaps writing her own details on there if she wanted), thus establishing a social connection, but over time the pile of cards gathered dust, all duplicates. It is unclear whether remarks had been made about Edith that she had overheard, or if her confidence failed her, but either way she developed something she had not exhibited at any other point in her life: a shyness that bordered on (or perhaps was) social anxiety. It troubled her so much that the one calling card she did return, to Elizabeth Wright, Joe Wright's wife and a philologist, academic and author herself, she only managed to because Ronald walked her to the door and rang the doorbell himself before fleeing round the corner. But it was fortunate that he did, for the Wrights swiftly became family friends too.

Although she probably would not have admitted it, Edith seemed most at home with the somewhat iconoclastic figures in Oxford: Elizabeth and Joe, and the young female academics that her husband tutored. Where class backgrounds and life experiences were muddled she felt most at home, as she had in the Primrose Society. But opportunities to socialise outside of this scant group of friends were barely existent for her, so she became terribly lonely in Oxford. She had but two solaces: the first, her piano. It had been brought out of storage when they moved into a rented house and the ability to play once again, in a house which she was the head of, whenever she wanted, soothed her immensely. The second solace was her family. She loved Ronald deeply, Jennie still provided her erstwhile support, and both she and Ronald were kind and loving parents to young John, and they were expecting another child soon, for Edith found out she was pregnant again in 1920.

Perhaps it was this that motivated Ronald to throw his hat into the ring for the role of English Language Reader at the University of Leeds, under one Professor George Gordon, a former Oxford English School man himself. Tolkien did not expect to be considered, but to his surprise he was offered an interview with Gordon in Leeds. The professor met him at the station, and, at first, conversation between them was awkward. However, as Tolkien recalled later, things picked up when he was asked about Sir Walter Raleigh, an Oxford English Literature professor at the time. Tolkien described him as 'Olympian' ('though I only really meant that he reposed gracefully on a lofty pinnacle above my criticism' – Tolkien considered him to be a poor lecturer).[5] He knew the job was his before he left Leeds.

Moving yet again was of course difficult for the Tolkiens. By this time, Edith had given birth to her second son, Michael Hilary Reuel Tolkien, on 22 October 1920. Although there had been fewer complications than John's birth, both she and he would not be well enough to travel for quite some time, so – as much as it pained him to be away from his family, especially with a newborn son – Ronald had to take rooms in Leeds alone at first.

However, it was not all bad; in spite of their differences on the subject of Sir Walter, Professor Gordon proved to be a kind and supportive manager. There was no room for Tolkien when he first arrived, so Gordon split his own office space with him, quite a feat as the small room was already shared with a French professor. Also, he gave Tolkien exactly what he wanted and craved at the time: autonomy and independence as an educator, for Gordon left much of the language side of the department under Tolkien's responsibility. Gordon had opted for the 'Oxford model', where English language and literature were one department with different specialities, and courses that provided exposure to both. The language side of the department was brand new, and it was up to Tolkien to build it up.

He relished the challenge, and once Edith, Jennie and the boys were comfortably ensconced in their new family home in Leeds in late November, he set about it with gusto, throwing himself into teaching and academic planning. At first he was extremely worried about his students, thinking the working-class Yorkshire lads and lasses who made up his classes too dull to be educated (perish the thought that Joe Wright should ever have heard him say that!), but he quickly realised he had them all wrong, and developed a profound fondness for his student body. This was in no small part due to a stark difference between them and a large contingent of the Oxford crowd; unlike the majority of the pampered, middle class students who preferred roustabouting to their education, the Yorkshire students were prepared to work.

With a student body already responding enthusiastically to their keen professor, the final element Tolkien needed was further support. George Gordon was a fantastic person to work for, but he needed more persons to champion his cause. Enter E.V. Gordon (no relation), a Canadian scholar and a recipient of the prestigious Rhodes scholarship at Oxford. Founded in 1902, the Rhodes scholarship is a sizeable award for international students, and one of the first of its kind. Gordon had in fact been tutored by Tolkien not two years before.[6] E.V. Gordon, much to Tolkien's delight, had more in common with his Yorkshire students than Tolkien himself. He was fiendishly hardworking, an attribute that led to him becoming Tolkien's long-time collaborator and friend. His diligent nature complemented Tolkien's enthusiastic if flighty attention span, and together they worked on numerous texts, including *Sir Gawain and the Green Knight*. E.V. also brought Old Norse and Icelandic to the course. Furthermore, together he and Tolkien founded the 'Viking Club', an informal society for English students and faculty to write their own Old English poems, read Icelandic sagas, and drink beer in good company.

This, plus their innumerable efforts as teachers and curriculum designers caused their student body to swell, going from eight students to twenty in only a few short years, making them a third of the English faculty as a whole.

Their efforts did not go unnoticed; although Tolkien did not receive George Gordon's professorship when he returned to Oxford in 1922, he was assured that a new professorship would be created for him, in recognition of his achievements and integral role in the English faculty. And so Tolkien became Professor of English Language in 1924. However, he did not stay in Leeds for long. In the early months of the next year, the Rawlinson and Bosworth Professorship of Anglo-Saxon (here meaning Old English) opened up in Oxford, and Tolkien, not imagining himself to be considered much of a candidate at his relatively young age for English-style professorships, decided to apply. To his surprise, he was considered. The faculty ended up voting in a tie between him and Kenneth Sisam, another highly respected professor (and Tolkien's tutor a decade before), at three votes apiece. It was left up to the vice chancellor to cast the deciding vote, and – after recommendation from George Gordon – he plumped for Tolkien.[7]

And so, less than a year after Tolkien had been awarded his professorship in Leeds, he was offered the much more prestigious professorship in Oxford, and was made a fellow of Pembroke College. Thoroughly stunned that he had got the position, he wrote an extremely contrite letter to the University of Leeds explaining why he was tendering his resignation so soon. Although sad to see the man who brought so much new life into the English faculty go, Leeds was understanding, granting Tolkien's newly vacated professorship to the more than capable E.V. Gordon, who flourished in the role.

With the Leeds chapter of his life ending, and Oxford-bound once more, if he were to reflect on his time at Leeds it would only be fondly. He had written and published several poems there, in a verse collection published by the English Department *Northern Venture*, in the *Yorkshire Poetry* serial and then in the Leeds University magazine. Not only had he grown into his full academic ability there, but the community in Leeds was far more welcoming and harmonious than that of Oxford. For one thing, Edith found herself right at home in Leeds. There was far less formality than in Oxford, and she made friends with several of the wives of Tolkien's colleagues, and regularly attended the events that the university would hold for faculty families. There were informal dances which she loved, as well as carefully thought out activities to include the children of the university staff. One such event was the annual Christmas party, where the vice chancellor would even dress up as Father Christmas to entertain the children. Certainly, this was a welcome inclusion, for the Tolkien family had grown bigger in Leeds: on 21 November 1924, Edith had given birth to her third son Christopher John Reuel Tolkien.

At the time, Edith was less than thrilled with this development. Although it was a less traumatic birth for her, she was still completely exhausted, and slightly frustrated at having a third boy and not a daughter. However, she loved the baby nonetheless, and Ronald was thoroughly overjoyed by him, writing of him with a great fondness. Even so early in Christopher Tolkien's life, Ronald seemed to have identified Christopher as the kindred spirit he would grow up to be. For without Christopher's lifelong passion and work on his father's fantasy world, we doubtless would not have Middle-Earth as we know it today.

Chapter 11

A Long Spell in Oxford, Hwaete

After Leeds had welcomed him with such open arms Ronald felt almost guilty to leave it, and to uproot his family once more, but Oxford was where more career opportunities beckoned. So, once again, the family upped sticks and moved back to Oxford in 1926.

They settled on Northmoor Road, in an L-shaped house that was number 22, where they would live for another four years, before moving to the larger 20 Northmoor Road in 1930. When Edith, Ronald and the three boys first moved into Northmoor Road, Edith was apprehensive. She desperately wanted something like the informal, welcoming atmosphere of Leeds, but Oxford still felt closed to her. The problem was further compounded by the way in which they moved. Ronald had visited and purchased the modest L-shaped property before Edith had even seen it, because she was caring for the children, who had caught ringworm from a photographer's comb. Upon seeing the house when she and the boys travelled down to live in it, Edith declared it too small for a family of five. The problem would only compound later when she fell pregnant again, although Edith was this time delighted with the result. Finally, she had the daughter she wanted: baby Priscilla. At last, their family felt complete, and not long after, they moved into the larger house at Northmoor Road.

As for Ronald, he was throwing himself into his work. He was young for a faculty professor, and thrust into navigating the tricky politics of the Oxford collegiate system. Most fellows were meant to show first loyalty to their college, with the exception of faculty professors, who showed loyalty to their department, but were still assigned a college. This led to some tension between the two groups, as colleges sometimes felt that they had faculty professors foisted upon their pre-existing social groups. Tolkien's own college, Pembroke, often felt unwelcoming to him. And that was to say nothing of the dynamics of the English department itself; the rift between English language and English literature was a strong as ever, and the syllabi just as hotly contested. Meetings sometimes led to raised voices and harsh words. Nonetheless, he was a diligent professor, passionate about his role as an educator. Oxford required its professors to teach a subject with a minimum of thirty-six lectures per year; in his first year Tolkien gave over 130. He very much believed in a rounded approach to his subject of 'Anglo-Saxon' (Old English languages and cultures from 450 AD to the Norman conquest, both called 'Anglo-Saxon' at the time in spite of the term's vagaries and inaccurate implication of monoculture), but also initially he had few fellows to support him, so he taught the subject to the best of his ability, largely solo.

Much like in Leeds, Tolkien quickly gained popularity with the student body. Perhaps the best known and popular of his achievements at the time were his lectures on *Beowulf*. These were general lectures which did not require a specialist understanding of Old English to attend or enjoy, and he would often pack out a large lecture theatre with eager and fascinated students, waiting for him to start the lecture in Old English, with the first line of *Beowulf* itself, 'Hwaete!' Through context, students took this to mean 'quiet', when it fact it simply means 'indeed'.[1] The *Beowulf* lectures left a startling impact on those who heard them. As his former student and long-time friend, W.H. Auden wrote to Tolkien years later on his *Beowulf* oration, 'that was the voice of Gandalf'.[2]

In fact, Tolkien is considered one of the seminal *Beowulf* scholars, responsible for elevating its place in the syllabus and its cultural impact on British history. However, there is a large flaw in his reading of the text, and thus in his extrapolated academia. When Tolkien discusses *Beowulf* he talks about the epic's singular author. This is flawed for a number of reasons. First of all, as a myth, told and retold over generations, *Beowulf* is not in any way comparable to a singularly authored text. *Beowulf* is the unconscious work of a collective; it has the thumbprints of multiple cultural voices all over it, pulling the narrative's meaning this way and that. The most striking of these obvious breaks in cultural meaning is that of the impact of Christianity. *Beowulf* has survived as a piece of literature because it was transcribed by monks during the time when Christianity was establishing a firm stronghold in England over the pagan religions preceding it. *Beowulf* was a pagan folk epic, but the monastic record of it changes details, shifts narrative beats, and bends the tale to include the intervention of a Christian God at critical moments of the plot, as well as the detail that Grendel is a descendent of Cain.

Perhaps then Tolkien was discussing the single Christian author, the one scribe who added to the Cain myth as he chose... but again, there was no singular author. The surviving *Beowulf* manuscript was transcribed (and added to, and edited by) two different tenth-century scribes. They have different handwriting on the manuscript as well as different writing styles (the second scribe is more faithful to whatever record they were originally transcribing from).[3] This leads to a confusing oversight for such a diligent scholar as Tolkien. It is possible that his own double life as a scholar and fiction author clouded his judgement on this. *Beowulf* was not the only myth he talked of in terms of singular authors. It is possible that his belief in a mythic truth, that the word of Catholic God is filtered through all world mythologies past and present, also confounded his academic vigour. In his mind, if all myths had roots in the divine, it seems to be as a singular divine inspiration, rather than a presence of godliness around storytelling in general. To Tolkien, stories and myths have the same origin, a spiritual inspiration to a singular author, who then interprets this divine message as is his wish. This led Tolkien not only to believe in the positive ideal that spiritual nourishment could be found in all fiction, but also a narrowing of his scope; there were only ever single writers, and he only ever acknowledged male ones in his lectures, and their stories' inspirations were metaphysical rather than observable. Perhaps this was why he also pushed so hard against analytical views of his work, as to him to directly trace only to the mundane inspirations for stories leaves out their most important one.

Furthermore, the example of *Beowulf* raises an important point on the study and analysis of Tolkien as an author and scholar. Namely, that the two cannot – and should not – be separated. To discuss them as two individual entities, 'Tolkien the scholar' and 'Tolkien the author', is an often-made and deeply flawed distinction. His academia and his fiction writing were not just closely linked, but tightly interwoven. His linguistic analysis and research lent Quenyan, Sindarin and Khuzdhul their linguistic integrity. His analysis of ancient poems and myths gave the stories of *The Silmarillion* their weight. His knack at world building came directly from his own extensive research on ancient cultures, made other only by time. And, crucially, his background as a fiction writer hugely influenced his academia. He was inclined towards creative approaches, dedicated to breathing life into the texts that he analysed, letting them live again as fiction and performance pieces, not just things to be dissected. His writing style was more vivid than his contemporaries, painting his explanations with simile, metaphor and engaging example, eschewing the forced sterility of philological texts that had become vogue. But conversely, he was liable to fall into projection, imagine ancient creative processes to be similar to his own, their voices to be singular, and startlingly akin to his.

Aside from his directly academic work (lectures, marking papers, arguing for revisions on how the subject was taught, tutoring), he also filled his time with a variety of social activities. He dined out in halls at least once a week. He founded a club called the Coalbiters (or *Kolbítar*), in which he and some other academic friends learnt and translated Icelandic poetry together. Tolkien had founded the club with the goal of showing his friends that ancient epics were worth reading in the original Icelandic, so he was only one of the two members who were fully fluent. The other was the Icelandic language don Dawkins. Among the other members was a man named C.T. Onions, who Tolkien knew from his days with the dictionary team, and a medievalist who went by the name of Jack. Jack, a scruffy man who was only 27 when he joined the English department, had fast become one of Tolkien's closest friends. He was another large part of his social life, for – aside from the clubs they both frequented, the Coalbiters and later the now famous Inklings – they met up every Monday for a beer together, attended dinners in halls together, and Jack also visited the family home. The children enjoyed his company tremendously, for he did not patronise them and brought them E. Nesbitt books.

Aside from (and a part of) the social time they spent together, they also contributed to each other's work and personal lives tremendously. The influences on each other can be seen in their published works, for to people outside of his close friends, Jack was known by another name: C.S. Lewis. Lewis and Tolkien (or Jack and Tollers to each other) had a decades-spanning friendship, which started here and would vary dramatically in its tone and warmth. But now, in Oxford, in the English department and the Coalbiters, they were bosom buddies.

When they first met, at an English department meeting, they were unsure what to make of each other. Tolkien, the slender, plainly dressed but presentable philologist, a devout Catholic who lived in a townhouse with his wife and four children, was almost a complete opposite to medievalist and literature side newcomer C.S. Lewis, scruffy in his unpressed trousers, a bachelor living in halls, and an agnostic. They also did not initially spark it off, as Lewis' diary entry after meeting Tolkien for the first time demonstrates: 'No harm in him: only needs a smack or so.'[4]

But they soon realised they greatly enjoyed each other's company. Tolkien was instrumental in Lewis' return to Christianity, converting him from a non-believer to a person of unspecified faith to a Christian, though never (much to his frustration) to a Catholic. The turning point for Lewis to return to Christianity was a night-long talk with Tolkien and a mutual friend about Lewis' complex feelings towards Christian mythology over pagan mythology. As Lewis' two friends navigated Lewis' contradicting and inconsistent feelings, he realised he was placing a burden of purpose on Christianity that he was not placing on other religions, catalysing his conversion, and further cementing his friendship with his Tollers.

But there is another side to this patient, doting and friendly Tolkien, willing to engage in intellectual debate and invest time in one he loved. During a lot of his time in Oxford, but especially during the very close companionship with Lewis, Ronald neglected the already isolated Edith. Much written of Tolkien in this time focuses on Edith's lack of further education as the sole factor at play, but that is a narrow view of their domestic situation. Even when talking of the other professors' wives who occupied some social status, it is all written in terms of how their best option to be included is for them to work to support their husbands in more and more ways. Wives with an education had often been the pupils of their husbands, and this included the spouses of relative progressives within the system, such as E.V. Gordon and Joe Wright. That kind of relationship was less disturbing in its implications than it would be today, as many of these women were in the first generation of their family and even social circle to have access to further education, and as such had limited options for partners who would accept them as intellectual, let alone intellectual equals. However, this relationship still inherits an implicitly imbalanced power dynamic: almost a form of academic wife-husbandry. (Wife husbandry is a fictional relationship trope where one partner – usually the husband – had a protective and/or nurturing role in the other partner's youth or even childhood, and the pair later marry. Husbandry here is used in the context of phrases such as 'animal husbandry' to imply that one partner is almost raising and training the other to fit that role.) This dynamic continues into the woman's academic career; if her academic voice was nurtured by the man into whose family she was also subsumed, are her academic achievements not *really* a reflection, or even an *extension*, of his? In relation to the Tolkiens' social circle, nothing is written of Lizzie Wright or Ida Gordon's achievements or social status or friendships in their own right, and times when there did seem to be a genuine informality and independence of social circles for the couple, such as Leeds, are glossed over quickly to get to the 'important' years when Ronald was writing his most popular books.

But back to Oxford. Edith's second option to be included in Ronald's world as an educationally neglected woman was to make her home a social hub for Ronald and his friends. But this required the excessively formalised networking which already made Edith terribly anxious, not to mention the 'prize' at the end seemed unappealing to her. Why should she turn her family home into a men's club for professors who barely spoke to her? This was another way in which Oxford fell short of Leeds; often bachelor professors and male students who came to visit Ronald had no idea how to talk to her and awkwardly shuffled past. The 'dull stodges' Ronald described in Leeds had been less isolated and raised with better manners, knew how to make small talk and did not shrink away from her when she asked how they were.

Mercifully, there were female students who became not only Edith's friends but friends of the whole family. These and other students who became a friend of the family had to learn how to navigate Edith and Ronald's 'unique' way of communicating. They would invite someone over to see both of them, and would speak simultaneously at them on completely different subjects. Edith would be asking someone for updates about their relative, whom they had last described as having failing health, whilst at the same moment Ronald was asking someone about a new piece of research into Icelandic poetry or similar. Although this was initially difficult to manage for many guests, they learnt to adapt, and after a while the couple and their children had a steady stream of shared visitors whom they would entertain simultaneously, if not together.

Edith and Ronald's dynamic in Oxford was nuanced. There was no doubt that Edith struggled with having friends of her own, and navigating the complex mores of Oxford social life, and that even without Edith playing hostess Ronald still brought many of his friends round, but she did still greatly enjoy Ronald's company, and him hers. Writing to his son decades later, Ronald described seeing or hearing things throughout his life, both in academia and the world around him, and immediately thinking that he must tell her about this event or sight.[5] There was a desire from him to include her in his world, but still with an element of distance. She was someone who mainly experienced Oxford University life through Ronald's second hand accounts, and the stories of their guests over tea, not from being invited to dinners or soirées herself. It is possible that some of this distance was intentional on Ronald's part; his favoured nickname for her throughout their courtship and married life was 'little one': diminutive and idolising without a place of equality.

From what we know of Edith during the Oxford years, it does not seem she always wanted to be Ronald's 'little one'. As a married woman who grew up in a unique household as an illegitimate girl, she did not know how to manage a household as a middle-class married woman was expected to. Uncertain and isolated from those who would share her experiences and perhaps help her, she fell into a pattern of a strict routine seldom deviated from. Meals were served promptly on Edith's chosen hours and Edith's chosen time; she kept all the clocks in the house wound to be five minutes fast, and demanded the rest of the family keep time in a similar way. Breakfast was at 8 o'clock 'Edith time' every day, and the whole family was expected to eat together for every meal, so if Ronald took the children for early Mass in the morning they would often have to make it back in double-time on their bikes. The children also had to return from their school for lunch, and – unless Ronald had a dinner out at the faculty – everyone was expected back for tea too.

It is easy to see how someone feeling immense pressure to live up to her peers became so dedicated to her routine, as a refuge or perhaps defence from gossip. What could any of these other Oxford wives say about her now, for she kept an immaculate house with an impeccable routine. However, as could be expected, this made employment of a housekeeper difficult. Edith cooked and managed most of the house herself, but (again, as was expected of middle-class women in her role at the time) employed a housekeeper to help with the cleaning. She worked through many housekeepers who did not meet her strict routine standards, until she employed Phoebe Coles, who ended up working for the household for many years. This is not to say that Edith didn't still feel keenly out-of-place.

Prior to their move to Leeds, Edith had felt deeply ashamed of their house in Oxford. And then, upon their return, the house Ronald had secured for them sight-unseen on her part was too small, but once they moved to number 20 Northmoor Road her fears abated somewhat, although she still never fully entered the circle of the Oxford wives. So aside from managing the house, she kept herself busy with other things. She kept an aviary, which she often walked into to calm herself. She decorated her tea room to her tastes, and of course kept playing her piano as a hobby. And she made a point of calling on Ronald regularly throughout the day if he was working in his study. This was partly to keep him abreast of the issues of the house, partly to check in with him, for their hours were by now completely different, and partly for simple company. Edith spent most of her day either with Phoebe or completely alone, so any time she could talk to Ronald was exciting for her. However, Ronald often found these short conversations an annoyance, and recorded them in his diaries from the time as a frustration. Some biographers have made much of him 'tolerating' Edith's company, seldom acknowledging Edith's patience and tolerance for his erratic schedule, and emotional distance from her in favour of his male friends.

However, one matter Ronald and Edith were completely united on was their family. The couple loved their children deeply, and tried hard to give them the loving, supportive, and consistent home life neither of them had as children. The family went on holidays to beaches together, including to Lyme Regis where the by now grandfatherly Father Francis would join them, playing with the children as he had Ronald and Hilary decades before. A huge focus for the family was quiet evening time together, for which Ronald would perform 'winter reads' for the children: reading aloud from their favourite stories, or creating some of his own. Ronald also began writing increasingly elaborate letters to the children from Father Christmas, which became so detailed and were so loved by the family that they were published posthumously as *Letters To Father Christmas*. This tradition became so elaborate that eventually Ronald roped in their local postman to deliver the letters, and – as the children found out, one-by-one who the real author was – they would become in on the secret, and work to not spoil it for the younger ones.

Throughout this time, Ronald had maintained his close friendship with E. V. Gordon since he had moved away, and Gordon had taken up the new professorship Ronald had been awarded. However, collaboration between them proved increasingly difficult. Tolkien always had several projects on the go at once, and lectures to prepare, and other things occupying his mind, and without the more focused Gordon physically sharing his office and inspiring him to commit to their projects with the same fervour, their collaborations were largely shelved. Of course, the logistics of collaborating by post added a further level of difficulty the waywardly minded Tolkien was ill-equipped for. Nonetheless, they maintained regular friendly correspondence. E.V. Gordon met BA and PhD student Ida Lillian Pickles, a Medieval English and Old Norse specialist who he taught for a spell and then later married in 1930 (the year of her PhD graduation). Tolkien was overjoyed by the news and composed *Brýdleop* – an Old English praise-poem in Old Norse alliterative metre – as a wedding present, which delighted the happy couple.

In 1931, Gordon took the Smith Professor of English Language and Germanic Philology at the University of Manchester, so the family moved there. E.V. and Ida had four children, and life seemed to be going well for them, with Ida maintaining a degree of academic involvement with her husband's work at Manchester. They joined the shared friends of Edith and Ronald, and Ronald wrote to both Ida and E.V. regularly, even if the projects he and E.V. continually meant to get round to gathered dust.

However, things took a sharp turn for tragedy in 1938. E.V. Gordon was hospitalised with gallstones, and had them removed via routine operation, but there were complications, and he never made it home, dying suddenly a few days later, leaving Ida, their children, the Tolkiens and their other friends completely bereft. All of Ida and E.V.'s children were less than 7 years old when their father died, so Ida took on some of E.V.'s teaching duties, starting a lifelong involvement with Manchester University as a teacher and lecturer, which only ended with her retirement as a senior lecturer thirty years later. Additionally, she worked hard to complete several academic texts and translations E.V. had been working on prior to his death, and published them posthumously.

But Tolkien could not bring himself to return to the projects he and E.V. had worked on together. So much of Tolkien's writing was in response to profound grief; the losses of Rob Gilson and G.B. Smith and his mother have all had an echo or been explored in his later fantasy works, but there was something about losing E.V. Gordon, a collaborator, that was different. Although Ida finished and published their translation of *Pearl*, Tolkien instead searched for another collaborator and new projects.

This was not out of disrespect for his friend, in fact quite the opposite. Tolkien could not think of finding someone else who could work with him in the way E.V. had on their collaborations, and could not think of replacing him, yet felt he did not have the wherewithal to complete the projects himself. He was by now quite acutely aware of his work style; he had wonderful, lofty ideas and grand designs, but struggled to put them to paper, partly due to a lack of focus and partly due to a restless perfectionism. He delayed the publication of some manuscripts because he could not get his introduction right.

So he needed another collaborator. He found one soon enough in a Belgian former student of his, Simonne d'Ardenne, with whom he collaborated on her translation of *The Life and Passion of St Julienne*, with plans to collaborate on a translation of *Katerine*, but it was not to be. She had moved to Liège to accept a professorship, and soon the two academics found themselves up against an even greater foe which would disrupt their collaboration: the shadow of war. But before that, Tolkien's life and writing took a far more pleasant detour: to a hole in the ground.

Chapter 12

On Discovering Hobbits

The beginnings of one of the most popular children's books in the Western canon were – perhaps surprisingly – a humble mixture of boredom and inspiration. In order to maintain his comfortable middle-class lifestyle for his large family, aside from his work as a don, Tolkien also regularly marked examination papers of school-age children. Whilst this extra source of income was welcomed to finance the maintenance of the house, he typically found this terribly boring. As such, he often wrote notes on the backs of papers or blank pages included in the essays, not about their subjects, but on his private world. One day, when he was marking such a paper, he noticed the student had left a blank page, and – for some reason he could not place – he wrote on it, 'In a hole in the ground there lived a hobbit.'

As he would recall in later life, he didn't know why he wrote it, nor what hobbits were, but felt he needed to 'discover' more about them. This was how he discussed his fiction: not as creation, but as discovery. To him, the world of Middle-Earth felt real, not in a literal sense, but in that it contained worldly truths, as he argued all sub-creators hope their work does. As such, he treated much of his writing exactly as he treated his academia: not as creation but as research. Here, out of ennui, he had stumbled upon an unfamiliar word, now he must pour over his texts to uncover how to define it.

The mundane inspirations for hobbits and the other fantastical creatures Bilbo encounters are somewhat easier to trace. George MacDonald's goblins were the precursor to Tolkien's. A favourite book of his boys, E.A. Wyke-Smith's *The Marvellous Land of Snergs*, also delighted Tolkien as he read it to them. He was particularly taken by the Snergs themselves; a race of small helpful humanoid creatures with a fondness for feasting, all of which are traits hobbits would soon share. And finally, a wildcard; although Tolkien did not read much modern literature, he had read and liked the satirical novel *Babbitt* by Sinclair Lewis, in which the titular character is a comfortable middle-class man with something missing from his life and a fondness for nature, and who after a series of mid-life crises, returns to the mundane conformity of his home and social status. Eventually, the first hobbit Tolkien discovered would be Bilbo Baggins: a comfortable middle-class man with something missing from his life, a fondness for nature and an arc which resolves with him returning to his comfortable home. In an interview Tolkien even conceded that hobbits share *Babbitt's* 'bourgeoisie smugness'.[1] Though Bilbo never experimented with bohemia and socialism as *Babbitt* did, the circuitous nature of his quest and status is an echo of Lewis' satire, but played with complete sincerity, attributable to the seismic difference between the two authors' politics.

Hobbits also borrowed some of the linguistic aesthetics from *Babbitt*, as Tolkien was fond of the syllables, echoing them in Baggins and the word hobbit itself. But it would be a mistake to believe that *The Hobbit* is simply a mixture of two children's fantasy books, an American satirical novel and multiple myths blended together. Tolkien took inspiration from these works, certainly, but his discovery had something else to it: an inherent 'selfness'. Firstly, his main character Bilbo Baggins owes many of his idiosyncrasies to his author – from his fondness for ornamental waistcoats, rambling walks and the pipe, to his over fondness of the comforts of home. But then there are the direct nods to Tolkien's childhood, and even his own family. The unusual matriarchal Tooks, to which Bilbo's mother Belladonna and her two sisters belong, mirrors Mabel and her sisters. The fact that the Baggins' are considered more respectable folk, but several of them have a meanness to them, mirrors Ronald's perception of the Tolkiens. But most strikingly, Bag End, where Bilbo lives, is named after Jane Neave's farm, colloquially known as Bag End. The Shire itself is evocative of the West Midlands, in particular Tolkien's heart-home: the county of Worcestershire and the Sarehole of Tolkien's memory.

But there was even more than those surface level, conscious nods and references that Tolkien celebrated. The leaf-mould of his mind called back to all sorts of shadowy, half-remembered inspirations. The hiking holiday to Switzerland with Jane and Hilary, the stories of dragons he'd loved so much as a child, and the legend of *Beowulf* he studied as an adult all played their part. The treacherous mountain passes which lead to the Company of Thorin Oakenshield's misadventures in Goblin-Town, Smaug's weakness, and the theft of a cup from him by Bilbo. All clear parallels, but there is something deeper, and more uncomfortable in the first story of hobbits Tolkien penned. Although this was a story that started life for his children, there is a maturity of theme under the surface, particularly as the story progresses. Bilbo goes on an adventure that begins light-hearted and episodic, yet he is but a single player in a broader, much more dangerous story. The company is being pursued by Bolg, who is avenging his father Azog, and later the forces of the Goblin King, and they amass more and more enemies along the way. By the end, Bilbo has found himself in the midst of a bloody battle, but he is invalided away by a blow to the head. The same cannot be said for his friend and travelling companion of nine months, Thorin Oakenshield, who dies of his wounds after a deathbed reconciliation with Bilbo.

This is not to say that this is a direct parallel to Tolkien's experiences of the First World War, but that perhaps the themes the text explores – of gaining and losing friends, grief, adventure, and being a tiny player in a game far beyond your comprehension – were perhaps feelings that Tolkien needed to exorcise. Crucially, Bilbo has a guaranteed happy ending, a sense of peace.

But first and foremost, *The Hobbit* was a story for children: Ronald's children, specifically. Initially, it largely only existed as a 'winter read' for John and Michael at 22 Northmoor Road, with – to their recollection – a somewhat hasty ending. Indeed, the version John and Michael remember from the first Northmoor Road house probably never had a written ending, as Ronald got stymied on how to end it after the death of Smaug. Even that was entirely different to begin with; in the first draft, it is Bilbo who slays Smaug. The hobbit sneaks up on him and fatally stabs him in the belly. But as it was rewritten this detail was changed and dropped, and Bard the Bowman and the mythic song thrush take the place of this surreal dragon-slaying hobbit.

But the timeline of the writing of *The Hobbit* is difficult to pin down at best. John and Michael remember the number 22 Northmoor Road version; Tolkien himself insists he must have started it in the 1930s, after moving to number 20. What seems to be most likely is that the rough version that ended with Bilbo: Dragonslayer was started and then hastily resolved to appease his children, but the writing of the story proper was begun in earnest later. But even that version petered to a halt, and the story would have been left abandoned, and unknown outside of close friends and immediate family, were it not for two insightful former students.

Their names were Elaine Griffiths and Susan Dagnall. Friends, they had read English at Oxford together. Elaine was a remarkable academic and teacher, and in later life would go on to become one of the founding fellows of St Anne's Oxford, becoming one of the 'great teaching trio' alongside founding fellows Kirstie Morrison and Dorothy Bednarowska.[2] Elaine's postgraduate work in Old English Philology had been supervised by Tolkien, and she had become one of the family friends. So close to the family, in fact, that she was one of the few souls aware that Professor Tolkien had written a children's story about beings called hobbits. Tolkien even provided a recommendation for her to the publishing company she was now, in 1936, working on a revised edition of *Beowulf* for: George Allen & Unwin. This was where career-oriented Susan was now working. Susan had come up from London to meet with her friend Elaine, when Elaine raised Professor Tolkien's story with her friend, suggesting that Susan might want to look into it as a potential title for Allen & Unwin and recommended she borrow the typescript. Susan visited the Tolkien home that very day, and was given the typescript.

Reading it on the way back to London, she enjoyed it tremendously, with the exception of the abrupt ending after the death of the dragon. She returned the typescript to Tolkien, asking if he would consider properly finishing it as soon as possible, so that Allen & Unwin could consider it for publication in 1937.

Over that summer, Tolkien worked on *The Hobbit*, enlisting his second eldest Michael to help with typing up his handwritten copy as he was recovering from a school-window-related hand injury. With Tolkien beavering away at the ending, and Michael typing with one hand, the work was completed by early October and sent to Allen & Unwin.

The publishing house's chairman at the time was a man called Stanley Unwin. He had started working in the publishing company his uncle T. Fisher Unwin had founded, which Stanley turned into George Allen & Unwin after purchasing the controlling shares in George Allen & Sons in 1914. However, he was hardly a monopolistically minded man. He was a lifelong pacifist, and had refused to serve as a soldier in the First World War, joining the Voluntary Aid Detachment instead, providing non-military-associated nursing care to soldiers. His beliefs were reflected in the titles he published: works of fellow pacifists Bertrand Russell and Mahatma Mohandas Gandhi and avowed socialist and adult education advocate R.H. Tawney. Stanley Unwin cared deeply about the nature of the works he published, and – crucially – if they succeeded in their basic principle, for example, if a children's book would be considered interesting or good by children.

As such, he did not consider himself to be capable of being the final judge of *The Hobbit*, instead enlisting his 10-year-old son Rayner to read it and write a report. Rayner was compensated for his time and hard work with a shilling. His report was appropriately thorough and considered; he enjoyed the book thoroughly, he recommended a reading age of between 5 and 9, and he did not think it needed illustrations.

And so *The Hobbit* was to be published by George Allen & Unwin. Stanley only disagreed with Rayner on one issue, and asked for illustrations to be provided. Tolkien provided them, though he was decidedly unconfident in them, joking that they only demonstrated that he could not draw.[3] However, Unwin approved of them, and after some revisions to the number of colours he used and some debating of the placement of maps (he wanted to put the map of Middle-Earth at the beginning of the book, and Thror's Map at the end, and Unwin wanted both to be end pieces), the images were finalised. Following this, there were multiple revisions of the proofs, as Tolkien's perfectionism forced him to review and edit and alter his own work multiple times before he was happy. Primarily he removed a lot of immersion-breaking asides, having adopted the viewpoint that it was best not to talk down to children.

The Hobbit was eventually published on 21 September 1937. It received mostly positive reviews, particularly in the pages of *The Times Literary Supplement* and *The Times* itself. This was because the reviewer in question was C.S. Lewis, who regularly wrote for the *Literary Supplement* and managed to finagle a review in the paper itself too. Here we can see the benefit of Tolkien's environment, not only in how it inspired the text and world of his books, but in how it enabled his work to be elevated and shared. To put it simply: if Tolkien had not gone to Oxford, and had not become a professor, it is unlikely that anyone in the world would know of Middle-Earth. But here, in the life he led, with the privileges he enjoyed as an Oxford professor, he was put in the pathway of the brilliant Elaine Griffiths, the industrious Susan Dagnall, the iconoclastic Stanley Unwin and the rapturously supportive C.S. Lewis. This is not to diminish Tolkien's talents, of course, but he is the textbook example of someone whose elevated societal position allowed him to flourish to the fullest capacity. It would be disingenuous to present him as a simple man with a vision and a lot of luck; he had ample societal benefits in front of him, and because of them his work was able to reach a large audience many others could not.

And with this reach, the public responded. Very positively. *The Hobbit* became a children's bestseller, which initially slightly worried Tolkien as he was concerned that his colleagues might think that he was wasting his research time (in the end, he needn't have worried: for initially Oxford took very little notice of his hobby). Tolkien and Unwin decided to meet in person for the first time to discuss further matters. They were from entirely different worlds and felt it. (Tolkien compared Unwin to a Middle-Earth Dwarf, and considering the culture-clash between Bilbo and Thorin's Company should provide an indication of the stark differences between the two men.)

Differences aside, one thing was clear: children wanted to know more about hobbits, and Unwin wanted to know if Tolkien could provide the answers, in the form of a sequel. At first, Tolkien was surprised. *The Hobbit* had been written as a self-contained story, with its protagonist's arc thoroughly concluded by its end. That said, it was incorporated into his wider mythos; did this mean he could finally finish and publish *The Silmarillion*? But that was not a story for children, which was what a sequel to *The Hobbit* should have been, surely, given what the market wanted? Tolkien was at a loss. He had never intended to be a children's author, merely a storyteller to his own children. His forays into children's literature prior to *The Hobbit* had all started life as bedtime stories for his children.

His first such story were the tales of Carrots, a red-headed boy who went on adventures, which he told to his son John to help him get to sleep as he was troubled with nightmares. The Carrots stories were lost to time, as were the adventures of Bill Stickers, a roguish character invented to entertain Michael (inspired by a sign Tolkien saw which read 'Bill Stickers will be prosecuted'). Bill was a lawless sort, constantly hunted by his nemesis, who also owned his name to a road sign, Major Road Ahead. There has been speculation about the true origin of Bill Stickers' name, however.[4] Tolkien's friend C.S. Lewis was connected to and supportive of a secret society called the Ferguson Gang – a group of five women who teamed up to fight urbanisation by fundraising in secret for the (then starved of funds) National Trust, to the point of delivering bags of money and spending instructions to them in secret whilst wearing masks, or hiding it inside everything from cigars to a goose![5] The group's efforts were successful, and they saved around twenty buildings, but the interesting parts come from the group's pseudonyms. They were: Kate O'Brien the Nark, Sister Agatha, Red Biddy, Lord Beershop, and... Bill Stickers, and 'Bill' and Lewis corresponded. Whether Tolkien was inspired by this Bill Stickers, or tales of her from Lewis, or whether this was a coincidence is impossible to divine at this point, for Tolkien was a conservationist also, yet as far as we are aware did not correspond with the gang.

Other children's stories and characters by Tolkien are much easier to trace. A particularly miserable holiday at Filey beach, Yorkshire in 1925 and a motor accident in 1932 inspired two of his stories: *Roverandom* and *Mr Bliss*. *Roverandom* was initially told to console Michael, who had lost his toy dog on the beach that day. It is the story of a dog who is turned into a toy by a wizard, picked up and beloved by a boy, then lost at the beach, turned back into a dog by another wizard and eventually travels to the moon to have all sorts of adventures there. *Mr Bliss* – a whimsical nonsense tale of a man with a fantastical creature for a pet, whose bad driving leads him to (among other things) a trio of bears – was in part inspired by Tolkien himself driving into a stone wall in 1932, though Joan Tolkien (Michael Tolkien's first wife) also believes it was inspired by a trio of teddy bears owned by the boys, and Christopher Tolkien's favourite toy: a small car.

Either way, there was a surreal nonsense to both of these stories, and a much lighter tone than the high fantasy of his created world, and *The Hobbit*, which had now become a part of it. A part which now needed a sequel. At first, Tolkien was unsure what to provide, so he sent *Roverandom*, *Mr Bliss*, and some extracts from *The Silmarillion* to Allen & Unwin to see if they would suffice, or at least tide their audience over until whatever the 'sequel to *The Hobbit*' was to be. *Roverandom* was considered (and Rayner Unwin found it amusing), but its style was too far from *The Hobbit*, and so it was not published (although it was eventually published posthumously by HarperCollins in 1998). *Mr Bliss* was considered for publication, but it was calligraphically written and illustrated in such a way that it would be too expensive to produce as was, so Unwin recommended that Tolkien re-draw the manuscript with simpler illustrations. He never got round to it, and the book was once again only published after he'd passed on (by

Allen & Unwin in 1982). But *The Silmarillion* was the toughest needle to thread. Clearly for an older audience, Unwin sent it to a reader, who liked some elements, but remarked somewhat disparagingly on the names, misidentifying them as Celtic. Unfortunately, Stanley Unwin thought it wise to send the reader's report on to Tolkien, who took it to heart and was not much pleased, writing back at length that the names were not in fact Celtic and had been chosen with great care. Regardless, Tolkien felt that *The Silmarillion* was not wanted, and so continued to work on it privately, whilst trying to dream up a sequel to *The Hobbit*. And one would come of course, eventually, but Allen & Unwin had to wait twelve years.

It is interesting that in his first published book Tolkien's main character is a writer, the writer, in fact, of *The Hobbit*. One of the fascinating layers to Middle-Earth is the in-universe authors of the texts; Bilbo Baggins wrote *The Hobbit*, Frodo Baggins and Samwise Gamgee wrote *The Lord of the Rings*, and Elven scholars wrote *The Silmarillion* and so-on. Aside from adding an extra layer of depth to the text, it also seems to be an interesting writing exercise for Tolkien himself, to never give his voice as the omniscient narrator, and instead make a conscious effort to write his books from singular perspectives. Of course, Tolkien, as the discoverer of these texts, and not the author, is merely uncovering the writing of another as he would with an Old English or Icelandic text, and preserving that sense of voice was tantamount to keep Middle-Earth alive as a breathing world. Of course, this granted him a wonderful sort of 'get out of jail free' card if he ever wanted to change anything about his stories; for example, in the original printing of *The Hobbit*, Gollum willingly bets what would later become the One Ring Bilbo stole as a prize in their riddle-game.[6] In our universe, this is because the One Ring did not yet exist in Tolkien's head, and that was simply a magic ring (though it is important to note that Bilbo did steal it on both occasions). But when Tolkien finally had a more solid idea for what *The Lord of the Rings* was to become, he revised both Gollum's behaviour and the nature of the Ring into the chapter Riddles in the Dark as it is known now. But to write from Bilbo's perspective, why, what self-respecting hobbit, (a Baggins of Bag End, no less) would *want* all of Hobbiton to know that he had stolen from such a wretched creature? Tolkien not only wrote imperfect characters, but he wrote from their imperfect perspective, reflecting the complexities of both our world and theirs.

Chapter 13

The News Language of War

Tolkien is famous for being an author who lived through two world wars, yet very little is known about his active involvement in the Second World War. Biographers have a tendency to skim past this time in his life with little more than a few passing lines about it, if that, either because they were writing at a time before Tolkien having any involvement was known or because, even after some facts have been made public, a lot still remains intentionally shrouded in mystery.

What we do know is that Tolkien was profoundly heartbroken that his life, and crucially the lives of his children, were to be marred with war once again. Two of his sons would fight, and as before Edith would be consumed with worry as people she loved joined a war effort, unsure if they were ever to return.

In later life, after all the battles were won, Tolkien waxed philosophic on the difference between the two wars he lived through. To his mind, the First World War was fought by people, whereas, in contrast, the Second World War was a war fought by machines, leaving all of humanity in their wake as the only victors of a global-scale humanitarian disaster.[1] It could be said that those who lived through the horrors of what was meant to be the war to end all wars were loath to put their children through what they had endured, and so left much of the actual fighting to the machines. But this meant that people, soldiers and civilians, lost. There is a lot of truth to that sentiment, but there was another way this war was to be fought, and that was by subterfuge.

With the technological advancements in the areas of wire communication, sonar and radar were proliferating, there was more of an ability than ever before to pass messages back to superiors, or to intercept someone else's messages. Spying has been a part of warfare for as long as warfare has existed, but now it boomed into its own war industry, a major cog in a terrible machine.

And England was primed to capitalise on that. Spies were already recruited from Oxbridge as a matter of course. Undergraduates with a background in linguistics were wooed by British Intelligence, and primed to join up once they graduated, but in the war effort, the director of the Government Code and Cypher School (GCCS), a man by the probable pseudonym of 'Alastair G. Denniston', looked further afield, to the other academics and professors. Tolkien was one of fifty such persons earmarked.

It might seem natural that a polyglot like Tolkien would be selected, particularly because he not only knew multiple languages but was adept at finding the roots of code systems. However, one can imagine it must have been quite surreal for the National Recruitment team to put out the call to the man who was most known as a famed children's author for the past year and a half.

Tolkien answered the call, and attended a national spy training programme. For the longest time, all that was known of this was a passing reference to it in a letter to his publisher, as he was explaining why his 'sequel to the Hobbit' he was penning at the time was taking longer than expected.[2] Humphrey Carpenter explains in the following footnote that Tolkien attended a four-day training programme for potential spies, and for decades that was all the public knew of the situation.[3]

However, in 2009, new information came to light. He had attended, and passed, this brief GCCS training programme. Tolkien's GCCS training was the same programme Alan Turing (who would go on to break the Enigma code, essentially invent the computer and then be forcibly sterilised by the country he had diligently served for being homosexual) went through, and if he had accepted the GCCS offer he would have likely been positioned in the Bletchley Park code-breaking team, working under Turing on Enigma. His salary would have been £500 per year (closer to £50,000 in today's money) and it would have been a part of the war effort that was invaluable, but kept him away from direct action.

But Tolkien did not accept, and to this day we do not know why. This entire chapter of his life is shrouded with mystery, we are not even concretely sure of the number of days the GCCS training course took. Carpenter, the only biographer to date who has ever had access to Tolkien's own diaries, said four. The GCHQ (the English spy body the GCCS has now become, which released this information to the public after a confidential exhibit they held in the Gloucestershire headquarters for their recruits) says three. In his letter to his publishers, Tolkien himself says a week.

Naturally, we do not know what this training course consisted of, and the GCHQ historian who gave these statements (but remained unnamed for security reasons) could not elaborate on that, nor could he shed light on any of the mystery around the word 'keen' scrawled next to Tolkien's name, presumably by his instructor. Was he enthusiastic? If so, why did he not choose to join up? Or was it simply a pronunciation guide, to prevent the instructor from calling him Professor 'Tol-kine' or 'Tolk-ee-en'?[4]

Can we ever know why Tolkien chose not to be involved? The GCHQ historian joked in his statement that, 'Perhaps it was because we declared war on Germany and not Mordor.'[5] Although he may have prioritised his writing, of course in reality Tolkien was not so flippant: he had both responsibilities and people to worry about. Priscilla was a child and later teenager living at home throughout the war. John had travelled to the Catholic seminary the Venerable English College in Rome to start his training for the priesthood in 1939, but the war forced the seminary to move to England so he and the rest of the priests studied in Stonyhurst, Lancashire for the rest of the war. And Michael and Christopher both served in the army. Michael volunteered in 1939 but was told to finish studies at Oxford's Trinity College instead. He did, but by 1941 he had suspended his studies once again and rejoined the war effort, eventually receiving the George Medal for his contribution as an anti-aircraft gunner during the Battle of Britain, and met and married his first wife (nurse Joan Audrey Griffiths) during active service, before returning to Trinity College and his degree in Modern History in 1944, graduating the next year. By contrast, Christopher joined the Royal Air Force in 1943, trained in South Africa, and was commissioned into the RAF volunteer reserve at the end of January 1945, as a probation pilot only, where he served the RAF until he was transferred to the Royal Navy Volunteer Reserve at the end of June, before finally being promoted to flying officer 27 July 1945, less than two months before the end of the war.

Doubtless, although we can deduce possibilities for Ronald's motives not to become a spy, the trauma of the First World War, the responsibilities of his academic and literary work, and the feeling that he had never been the sort to thrive in any sort of war environment are all worthy candidates

– either in isolation or symposium – we are probably destined never to know for certain.

For Ronald, Edith and Priscilla, day-to-day life was almost unchanged. Oxford was fortunate enough not to have been a priority target for bombings, and the most major difference for the Tolkien family was that they now kept chickens (for extra eggs outside of rations), and used their garden to grow vegetables for the same reasons. Wood and metal were highly valued commodities during the war, making them hard to find, and so Tolkien made his chicken coops from scrap wood and bent and recycled nails.[6]

And that was that. Tolkien passed the rest of the war quietly, fortunate enough not to lose any immediate family to it. However, we do know that he was affected by the politics of Nazi Germany, when Rütten & Loening Verlag, a German publisher, inquired about his heritage, anxious that there were no Jewish ancestors in his line.[7] Tolkien and Unwin were rightly outraged by this antisemitism and Tolkien drafted two letters in response as they considered their options. The first, now oft-quoted by Tolkienists, was in Allen & Unwin's files, so was likely not sent, in which he replies, '… whether I am of Jewish origin, I can only reply that I regret that I appear to have no ancestors of that gifted people.'[8] The second merely clinically answered the mundane questions in the letter, choosing to ignore the inquiry about ancestry. It should be noted that, either way, that both Tolkien and Unwin were thoroughly disgusted by the notion, Tolkien writing on the matter to Unwin,

> 'I do not regard the (probable) absence of all Jewish blood as necessarily honourable, and I have many Jewish friends, and should regret giving any colour to the notion that I subscribed to the wholly pernicious and unscientific race-doctrine.'[9]

No German edition of *The Hobbit* was published during the time of Nazi power.

Although Tolkien took an admirable stance against antisemitism, it is unfortunate that this is not reflected in his work. Tolkien's Dwarves, drawing heavily on European legends loaded with antisemitism, although noble and kind, are also depicted as (and written about by Bilbo as being) focused on material riches, and decried for their cowardice (although this is thoroughly unsupported by the courage of the Dwarves in the text of all Middle-Earth books). And this is where Tolkien's dislike of allegory starts to break down. He may well have not intentionally written a story where White Scandinavian-coded Elves are viewed by the highest god of the world as inherently nobler than the Dwarves, Dwarves who – at one point in *The Silmarillion* – are hunted to the point of genocide of one of the Dwarf Houses by the Elves, because the Elves did not realise they were people, but that is what he wrote. His Dwarves also strongly physically resemble the antisemitic caricatures of Medieval Europe; they have exaggerated noses, ears, and facial hair. And by taking inspiration from legends, which themselves were conscious (and in the case of the Dwarves, malicious) allegory at some point in their history, he ended up writing stories with large antisemitic and racist undertones, which holders of similarly abhorrent beliefs have held up as examples of him being a secret supporter of fascism and Nazi race science, things he explicitly decried in life.

However, whilst it is of course admirable that Tolkien spoke out and challenged antisemitic readings of his work, his own worldbuilding calls into question whether he was truly unconscious in his use of antisemitic tropes to characterise the Dwarves. In Middle-earth, Moria is the Dwarven ancestral home in the Misty Mountains where they were first awoken by the Valar who created them. It was abandoned before the time of Thorin's quest in *The Hobbit* because the Dwarves mined deep enough to awaken a Balrog, a powerful fiery demon-like being. This is consistently framed in the books as the fault of the Dwarves for their 'greed.' The framing of tragedies and atrocities against a persecuted people being in some way self-inflicted due to greed in a very common antisemitic trope, but in addition to that, Tolkien's word creation leaves a clear and uncomfortable parallel to a real Jewish tragedy. As recorded in the Talmud, the First Temple built by King Solomon, and later the Second Temple, were on Temple Mount, a place of high ancestral and spiritual belonging for Jewish people.

The First Temple was destroyed by the Babylonian Empire, forcing the people into exile. After they reclaimed their homeland and built the Second Temple, the Roman Empire destroyed it, as a punishment for defiance of the Empire. Not only do these tragedies seem echoed in the Dwarven exile from Moria, solace at Erebor, and destruction of Erebor, but Temple Mount, its Temples destroyed by two separate invading empires, was also called Mount Moriah.[10] Whilst he was outspokenly against Nazism, a deeper dive into his work reflects the prejudices and bigotry he tolerated within himself and carried into his work, as we shall see.

Chapter 14

Writing in a Fallen Earth

At this point perhaps it would be best to take a step back and look at Tolkien solely from the perspective of his work. From Northmoor Road onwards, his external life does not change much for more than two decades. Many biographers have painstakingly pieced together the complex order in which Tolkien wrote his works at certain points in this stretch of years. Certainly, there are overt inspirations from his home life and children. However, there is a strange conundrum which occurs at this point in many a Tolkien biography, where the author struggles to answer the question 'how can such an excellent mind have lived such a mundane life?'

This misses the point. There is an inherent disrespect for the domestic within that question: as if being a husband and parent of four is presumed to have been a burden on Tolkien, a cage to his creativity. Frankly, to have read *The Hobbit* or *The Lord of the Rings* and to arrive at that conclusion is bizarre. It is text, not subtext, that the simple pleasures of comfort, security, safety and friendship are more precious than Mithril to both of those books, and it is not from a place of yearning for something unfelt. Bilbo's cosy life, Samwise's impassioned belief in the Shire as a way of life – not a place – that needs protecting, all come from a clearly deeply held belief of the author. Tolkien was a man who loved his wife, friends and children above all else, and took great pleasure in spending an unhurried cosy life with them. In fact, it is the thesis of both books that 'mundanity', 'cosiness' etc. is where the most good and remarkable things and people spring from. All the heroic deeds of Dwarves, Elves and Men from the First Age onwards would have been for nought if it were not for a strange old wizard putting his faith in a small cluster of sybaritic hobbits, and recognising their resilience and creativity within.

So if that is the central thesis, then why stop here to further discuss Tolkien and his work? Because there is more to Tolkien – and any author – than their central, conscious thesis, and this is especially true of a work as complex and dense as Middle-Earth. What else does Middle-Earth as a whole explore, and why?

As previously raised, there is faith. Catholic Christian God is a presence in Middle-Earth, as Ilúvatar, but he is not known to the denizens of the fictional world, nor most readers. Instead, faith in Middle-Earth concerns itself with the elements of Ilúvatar, or 'gods under God' as Garth calls them, who have been elevated by the pre-Christian nature of Middle-Earth to the position of a pagan pantheon.[1] Their angels are fallen demonic balrogs or daydreaming wizards. The deeply Catholic roots of Tolkien's world are hidden. Whilst this is a conscious choice by Tolkien, it is not a cynical one, based on broader applicability or perhaps whimsy; it stems from his academic passions. In the mythic past that Middle-Earth is set in, Christianity and the society that birthed it had yet to exist, so Tolkien returns back to that theme, the leaf-moulds of which were planted in his childhood, of mythic truth. In a metatextual sense, Ilúvatar is Catholic God. However, in the textual sense, he is the head of his pantheon of reflections of his different aspects. That all the characters Tolkien writes from the perspective of do not know of Catholicism, or the true nature of their under-gods, does not matter, for God's will is still present in Tolkien's sub-creation, irrespective of the characters' ability to perceive or recognise it for what it is. This was, as we have touched on in the previous chapter, how Tolkien perceived all of the world faiths both preceding and concurrent to Catholicism: people still interpreting the divine on a fundamental level irrespective of the additions or aesthetic addendums of other mythologies and faiths.

So in Middle-Earth we see paganism and Catholicism existing simultaneously without contradiction, and the comforts of home as the thing of highest value at the end of the quest. Surely, then, we have interpreted and divined all that needs to be said of Tolkien. But to leave interpretation of his works at faith and comfort is to sell him profoundly short. Underpinning all of Middle-Earth is an often understated but ever-present sorrow. Middle-Earth is a fallen world.

Fallen here means fundamentally imperfect in an irreparable way. Not necessarily by original sin, but by an evil: Melkor, the Valar who challenged Ilúvatar, and the discord he created. It is somewhat reductive to read Melkor as a simple Lucifer analogue; Middle-Earth's paganism shares fundamental truths with Tolkien's interpretation of Catholicism, it is not the Genesis myth with the names changed. Although Melkor covets Ilúvatar, his focus is more on the wish to create, and his sin is defiance and refusal of instructions. He creates discord in the world very literally, playing his part in the cosmic music of fate with loud trumpet blasts that jar with the structured music of the rest of creation. The world itself was formed as a musical battle of creative differences between Melkor and the rest of the Valar. The world was made fallen, or imperfect.

The world for Earth in the Middle-Earth texts is Arda, and fallen Earth is Arda Marred. What is notable about Melkor (and where the fully satanic analogue breaks down) is that Melkor is far crueller than most interpretations of Christian Lucifer, and represents a more mundane evil. Melkor's greatest atrocities were how he harmed the animals and people of Middle-Earth. He bred and/or transformed wolves into Wargs through methods unknown to any of the Middle-Earth characters who write about them, but how he made Orcs is the true monstrosity.

Whilst the wolves who became his Wargs were arguably tricked and transformed, the true history of the Orcs is intentionally obscured in the text and much more horrifying once it is picked out in the relief. In the First Age, some Elves were 'lost' as they travelled Arda Marred. Later, Orcs appeared. Their bodies bent and shrunken, their Elven perfection physically, brutally removed from them, and twisted against them to the point where Elven magic now burns them. If Elves are men who did not fall, then Orcs are men who were dragged down deeper, into a crueller fate than mankind was meant to understand. In a world created by a profound lover of languages, Melkor strips all Orcs of language after he 'creates' them. The Orcs are evidence of Melkor's greatest cruelty: a complete disregard for the lives of others. He wanted creations of his own so he stole away Ilúvatar's children and broke them. He wanted an army so he repurposed the Orcs like discarded toys.

The Orcs themselves represent a repurposed trope of their author. The Orcs are a fantastical stand-in for the 'savage race' archetype beloved by Tolkien in the books he read as a child, which springs from the systematic dehumanisation of non-White people in colonial literature (and beyond, as these concepts are reused without question for generations), designed to justify (or perhaps assuage the guilt of) the White conqueror populations that brutalised and enslaved Indigenous communities globally. Whilst Tolkien's choice not to follow this whole cloth shows some awareness that casting a race of humans in this role is wrong, the Orcs still play this role in the text, which leaves its implications as they were in the preceding fictions. The phrases 'slant-eyed', 'swarthy', 'black', 'black-skinned', and 'sallow' are used to describe Orc and half-Orc characters in Tolkien's work. These words were and are used in reality to dehumanise Black and East Asian people, in the context Tolkien uses them they were loaded pejorative terms when Tolkien was writing and they remain so now. To be clear: this is not an attempt to guess Tolkien's intent, merely a study of the after effects of his work. The 'savage race' trope is borne from violence; a systematic dehumanisation of very real people to hide a plethora of genocides and mechanised abuses against oppressed communities, and to turn these crimes into justified punishment (or tragic last resort) of the oppressor heroes. To recreate it without analysing the impact of it tacitly endorses a reductive view of deplatformed groups.

Additionally, there is how Tolkien portrays non-White humans in his works. The Haradrim are Tolkien's approximation of north-east African cultures, and the Easterlings were his approximation of Middle Eastern and Mongolian societies. Both fighting on the side of Sauron and the poor pressganged Orcs he inherited from Melkor. They are by turns outwardly evil, and by turns horribly naive to the intentions of Sauron, and the victims of circumstance. What they are not is fully realised in the way that the White humans of Middle-Earth are. They do not get to have complexity or agency, and are destined only to be victims of their own or Sauron's moral failings.

Tolkien's resistance to critiquing racism might have something to do with how he viewed the world. He placed great stock on the importance of heritage and proper place. To him, to step outside your societal role, assigned to you by your class, was bad for you and your community. This led him to have a sense of security in his own life and the lives of others that made him friendly with people from all class backgrounds, but also made him reductive in his views of other cultures and communities. There was his gallophobia (a fear of France and French culture) which spread even to cooking. He became very frustrated with foods that were not plain and unrefrigerated and English, a strange set of beliefs for an avowed Apolaustick to have. And he and Lewis both loathed the dandies and aesthetes, a culture which still persisted in Oxford even after the fall and passing of its most iconic figure, Oscar Wilde. To avoid being mistaken for aesthetes (and therefore potentially homosexuals), both men made the effort to dress plainly (or, in Lewis' case, badly: he refused even to press his trousers lest he be thought of as aesthetic in any way). Tolkien did allow himself one extravagance when he could: his ornamental waistcoats.

The debate about whether or not Tolkien was racist is ongoing in Tolkien academia to this day, but there is a reductive aspect to how it is framed. Tolkien defenders will point to individual examples of admirable beliefs Tolkien held, being both vocally anti-apartheid in his Valedictory Address to Oxford in 1959, and rightfully angered at the antisemitism of Nazi Germany, and hold these up as proof that he was never racist. But prejudice, in particular racism, is far more complex than that. Although he was not as racist as he could have been, there is still a pernicious xenophobia to the lore of Middle-Earth. Goodness is racialised as Whiteness, both in casting the Harradrim and Easterlings as villains and in framing the Elves as idealised Whiteness in features, skin tone and their version of civilisation and culture. In fact, cultures themselves are put on a hierarchy, those inspired by English and Scandinavian folklore and peoples at the top, those inspired by the caricatures of Indigenous American, Black African and Middle Eastern cultures swept up in the 'savage' trope at the bottom. Pidgin languages and creoles (such as the ones Orcs speak in Middle-Earth, and many different colonised societies spoke and speak today) are viewed as lesser, even as 'mutilated' language, when Tolkien could have used them as a symbol of reclamation of language by the Orcs: that after having been denied it by Melkor they sampled many to create languages for themselves after his fall. Tolkien's distaste for pidgin languages and creoles seems strange for a philologist whose specialty was a form of dialect English, itself a form of creative expression and language play divergent from standardised language, in other words, a less complex form of creativity and inter-community expression found in pidgin languages and creoles.

There have been arguments made that there are progressive ideas about race in Tolkien's Middle-Earth books. Professor Emerita Jane Chance argues that there are progressive ideas in support of diverse communities and inter-racial marriages in Tolkien's work, pointing towards the unions between Elves and Maiar and Elves and Men, and the diverse communities between Dwarves, Elves, Men and Hobbits as a result of the events of both *The Hobbit* and *The Lord of the Rings*.[2] However, as she also points out, this is inspired by Tolkien's interest in medieval texts about bonds between people from different regions of England. Therefore, Tolkien's work seems to draw a line in the sand with regards to who it is beneficial to mix with. In *The Hobbit*, Dwarves and goblins are mentioned as occasionally working together on mines, though this is framed as Dwarves who participate in this as lacking in moral fibre, not something to be celebrated. Similarly, characters with both Mannish and Orcish heritage are treated with suspicion and hostility, implied to have sold out the hobbits in Bree in *The Lord of the Rings* (with their facial features described in lurid racist caricature), whilst Half-Elven characters such as Elrond are celebrated. The union between a Maiar and an Elf which creates the Sindar race of Elves in *The Silmarillion* is also a poor reflection of interracial dynamics. Given the Maiar's status in Middle-Earth as the equivalent of angels, and set in the mythic past even by Middle-Earth standards, this reads more like a myth to justify the high status of White-coded Sindar, who fall near the top of the inter-Elven race hierarchy of Middle-Earth, establishing themselves as the ruling class over the Silvan Elves who do not have pseudo-angelic ancestry. Again and again, there is a hierarchical view of race and inter-racial relationships clearly present in the text of Middle-Earth. Needless to say, hierarchical views of races are inherently both racist and flawed.

These prejudices in Tolkien's writing come from his internalised views, what he thought and believed, and also his environment and time. For better or worse, he is rooted in Oxford and in the idealised Sarehole and Aletsch Glacier of his mind. That is what was idyllic and comforting to him, so anything new or outside of that was not welcome.

Chapter 15

The Story Rings True

Throughout this time, Ronald was of course trying to follow Sir Stanley Unwin's wishes and write the next hobbit story. But that proved much, much more difficult than he had imagined it would. For starters, *The Hobbit* was meant to be self-contained. Its protagonist had reached the end of his arc, and had little left to tell. Secondly, initially Tolkien had little use not just for Bilbo, but for hobbits as a whole. He had incorporated *The Hobbit* into his grander mythos as he had written it, but hobbits themselves still felt relatively modern to him and not suitable for the grander acts of heroism his world asked for. After all, what could hobbits do? They were plain, simple sybarites who disliked travel, the most adventurous one of which had ended his story rich and contented and happy and with no desire to adventure again. This left Tolkien completely stymied about where to go next.

Of course, there was one collection of stories that were deeply close to his heart: those that would become *The Silmarillion*, but those were not suitable for children, and Unwin's delight in *The Hobbit* had been about it as a children's bestseller, not... whatever *The Silmarillion* was. After having sent extracts of *The Silmarillion*, and the whole of *Roverandom* and *Mr Bliss* to Allen & Unwin, and receiving the feedback he did on *The Silmarillion*, he returned to the question of what else he could do with hobbits.

At first, his motivation was a further disruption of Bilbo; perhaps he had spent all of his troll-chest of gold and needed to set out on another adventure once again. But his sub-creation resisted him, and the elderly sybaritic Bilbo was not to be budged. The ending of *The Hobbit* had promised him a peaceful life, and Tolkien was not to disrupt it. So he gave Bilbo a son to go on adventures. This theme of a father and son team was one he explored in a never-finished story he had written after a discussion with C.S. Lewis, in which the pair agreed that one of them should try to write a time travel story and the other should try to write a space travel story. Tolkien's was time travel, and the story, *The Long Road*, was included in the papers Tolkien sent to Allen & Unwin in 1937. In it, a father and son travel back in time along the etymology of their paired names, eventually reaching Tolkien's Atlantis equivalent: Númenor. Númenor would later be incorporated into *The Silmarillion*, but this father and son would not, and later, Bilbo would be stripped of his son and have him replaced with a nephew. Around this time of Tolkien's writing there is a recurring theme of Tolkien attempting to incorporate father-son duos and then abandoning them.

It seems as if he was inspired by his own experiences as a parent to include this dynamic, in particular his relationship with Christopher, who was the most enthusiastic about Middle-Earth out of all his children, but it is unclear why he gave up on exploring these dynamics in his fiction. Fathers and sons are closely connected in Middle-Earth; many characters introduce themselves with the epithet 'son of [father's name]', and family history is important to Elves, Men and Hobbits. But these fathers do not travel with their sons, even those who existed concurrently, such as Thranduil and his son Legolas. Close father-son bonds are even a theme in the adversarial characters; the Orc Bolg marches out against the Dwarves of Erebor to avenge his father Azog, who was slain by Thorin's cousin Dáin Ironfoot. But there is still this repeated disconnect and separation between fathers and sons. Théoden's son died before his father's magically induced madness was lifted. Legolas is not present in *The Hobbit*, and Thranduil does not even travel to the Council of Elrond in *The Lord of the Rings*. Frodo is an orphan, and Sam leaves his father behind to go on the quest to destroy the Ring. Boromir and Faramir are explored as characters prior to meeting their father, and Denethor is only introduced as a character after the death of Boromir, his favoured son. Whilst it is often a common theme of fantasy for a character to leave family behind to go on a quest, or even for the family's death to be the main character's motivation to quest, what makes this striking in Tolkien's works is his multiple attempts to include father-son adventurers that never saw fruition, and the fact that often families in his work do quest together. Thorin's Company includes his nephews Fili and Kili. Frodo travels with his cousins Merry and Pippin. Niece and uncle Éowyn and Théoden fight on the battlefield together (albeit initially unbeknownst to Théoden). And, of course, husband and wife Beren and Lúthien work together through their lay to trick Morgoth.

There are many potential reasons why Tolkien ended up not exploring father-son relationships as he initially set out to. Perhaps the characters simply pulled away from that dynamic. Perhaps he found more fun in exploring the cousin and sibling dynamics that had been so formative to him as a child. Or perhaps there was a sense of very real fear to writing a father and son on an adventure. The grief of one half of that dynamic losing the other is certainly explored, and as someone who both lost his parents and lived through his sons seeing active combat that was surely on his mind.

Nonetheless, over time Bilbo's son became his nephew. At first, he was called Bingo, but over time Tolkien debated changing the name and then eventually changed it due to both the changing nature and tone of the story and having grown to loathe it. Bilbo's nephew was given the name Frodo, which had originally belonged to one of the cousin hobbit characters.

But still the story was somewhat aimless. What was the central conflict? What were these hobbits to do? Tolkien consulted his primary audience on the matter first: his children. Priscilla wanted to hear more about the Tooks, so the Peregrin 'Pippin' Took and the unusual matriarchal home life of the Tooks is further explored.[1] But this central problem still remained. Tolkien looked over *The Hobbit* for elements he had yet to explore, and he fell upon Bilbo's magic ring. This was an item that had entirely unexplored mysteries about it. He toyed with many ideas to do with the Ring's power, including the idea of making the Ring's power exact a price from the user every time, but not too much if the user's intent was good. But slowly, gradually, a new concept formed. Of a Ruling Ring, one of initially thirteen, until the idea was refined. And Tolkien began to fashion what was to become *The Lord of the Rings*, deciding on the title in 1938.

However, in this evolution something began to change. Although a true sequel to *The Hobbit*, the invention (or discovery) of Sauron and his Ring began to alter the work. The tone darkened, and the genre changed, moving farther away from *The Hobbit* and becoming closer to the sprawling epic of *The Silmarillion*. The hobbits became embroiled in a war. And the tale kept growing, and growing, becoming six books altogether.

But before then, there were further facets of Tolkien's world and life to be added to the work. He'd named a strange storytelling elderly man he and his family met on holiday 'Gaffer Gamgee', a reference to the gamgee tape of his youth, and now that character gave his name to Sam's father, Bilbo's loyal gardener. And there was one more important character to be added to the series.

Michael had a beloved wooden peg doll with yellow boots and a feathered cap call Tom Bombadil. Tolkien had made up stories about the doll to entertain the children. In an oddly foreshadowing moment reflecting how the Middle-Earth character of the same name would divide fans, Tom Bombadil the doll was disliked by Michael's brother John, to the point where the older boy once tried to flush him down the lavatory. He survived and was fixed and Tom Bombadil and his tales grew to become an important if enigmatic part of Middle-Earth.

Over the twelve years Tolkien dedicated to writing *The Lord of the Rings*, so many influences came and went, and although revisions were made, the whole remained largely intact, leading to a story with a shifting tone. Where *The Hobbit* starts and ends whimsically, the build up to the darker themes is more carefully managed; the episodic nature of the dangers Thorin's Company and their hobbit encounter racket up in danger as times goes on, so the transition to a dragon attacking a wooden town and the ensuing battle that blossomed from the two groups of refugees Smaug created and the Elves manipulating events for their king's interests is a surprising turn of events for the story but feels tonally anticipated. Whereas the first book of *The Lord of the Rings* is so light-hearted the shift to the broader story, in particular after the breaking of the fellowship, feels like a sudden plunge from security and adventure into real danger. One is not better than the other, but perhaps they represent the author exploring his feelings about seismic events in different ways.

Tolkien explores his trauma from the First World War in both, but in *The Hobbit* he is a veteran who survived, looking back on the futility and his grief at lost friends. By the time of writing *The Lord of the Rings* he has lived long enough to see the impact the 'Great War' had on the world, and crucially how that shock of the brutality of war and the lost generation did not last. The Second World War was happening whilst Tolkien was writing, and although he was not hugely directly affected, and was lucky enough that all of his children survived it, he could see the lack of progress from the First World War. His beloved countryside destroyed, either by factories or by bombs. His children at war. The permanent happy ending he had written for Bilbo may have felt horribly naive during those dark years.

So he rewrites. Bilbo's happy ending becomes a precursor for his nephew to lose all sense of safety and normalcy in a dangerous quest. The magic ring becomes a dangerous and evil artefact. And, crucially, the Shire is no longer an isolated place where adventure cannot happen, for our heroes don't return to the same place. They return to Saruman's revenge acted out on their people, and the order of the Shire in disarray.

There is a recurring motif of lack of safety in *The Lords of the Rings*. Nothing and no-one is safe. Gandalf dies to be reborn without a part of his personality that made him the beloved character he was. Boromir loses his heroism and then his life to the Ring and its forces. Frodo survives the quest, only to realise he can never truly return home after all he's endured as Ringbearer, and sails West soon after. Given Tolkien's experiences, it is not hard to see why. Although *The Lord of the Rings* was never a direct allegory for either of the world wars, it is a place where a man with a troubled mind exorcised some of his thoughts and feelings about living through both. As such, one can almost see, like the rings in a great oak, the phases the tone of the story took as he was writing prior to the war and during it.

There is much about *The Lord of the Rings* which speaks to the truly gargantuan task Tolkien imposed on himself in discovering this part of his world's history. Not only the sweeping explorations of danger, grief and hope, but also in the minutiae. At one point he did a series of rewrites to make sure he had accurately charted the phases of the moon for the whole journey. Every part of Middle-Earth must not only feel real, but be real: the phases of the moon, the times it takes to travel from one place to another, the food rations, the calendars, and of course what started it all – the languages. In many ways it is extremely fortunate that Tolkien's work has inspired fans who go to the lengths of learning the languages and charting the calendars and moon phases from the accurately recorded details in his books, for otherwise it could have been a horrible waste!

But before the success and the detail-driven fans there was the task of finishing the thing. By the time Tolkien was ready to publish, Britain had gone to and returned from war, and Rayner Unwin, who had been a 10-year-old child when he read and reported on *The Hobbit* for his father, had been a sub lieutenant in the Royal Naval Volunteer Reserve in East

Asia for three years. But now it was 1951, and Rayner had survived the war, returned to study English at Trinity College Oxford, and was now working in his father's publishing firm. It was at this stage in his life that he was sent the second of Tolkien's Middle-Earth books, the manuscript for what would become *The Lord of the Rings*.

As before, Rayner was delighted by the book, but unlike before he was now an adult in the publishing industry and as such was painfully aware of costs and potential audiences. He thought they absolutely should publish it, writing to his father to recommend as such, though they might lose a thousand pounds. To this Stanley Unwin replied: '*If* you think this to be a work of genius, *then* you may lose a thousand pounds.'[2]

The risk to Allen & Unwin Tolkien's epic represented was not to be sniffed at. As a sequel to *The Hobbit*, people were expecting another children's book, or something with a similar tone. At the time, sweeping pseudo-medieval adult fantasy fiction books did not really exist in the Western canon, and certainly they were not yet their own genre. They carried with them the unfortunate perception of being 'fairy tales' and therefore childish, or myths and therefore to be read as dry classics to be analysed, not as fiction to be enjoyed. No book sells itself; Allen & Unwin would have to put time and money into finding an audience for the behemoth, should one even exist. Then there was the sheer size of the thing. Tolkien wanted it to be split into six different books, which from Allen & Unwin's perspective was daunting and bizarre as some of the books were not narratively fulfilling in their own right and clearly part of a larger epic. Plus there was the problem of paper and ink still being rationed at the time during post-war Britain, when the amount of paper that could be wasted on a series of books that were paced oddly in the way the author wanted to present them, which had no proven audience, would seem like madness to any publisher.

Nonetheless, Rayner pushed for Tolkien's work to see print. Unbeknownst to him, Tolkien was also courting other publishers, specifically Collins. Over the years, the Allen & Unwin reader's lukewarm and largely confused response to *The Silmarillion* had morphed in Tolkien's mind into the company despising his 'private nonsense', and as he finished *The Lord of the Rings* he thought that the best course of action was for *The Silmarillion* to be published also. This had led to a long flirtation between a Collins staffer Milton Waldman and Tolkien, with regards to getting the whole of both *The Lord of the Rings* and *The Silmarillion* published in accordance with Tolkien's wishes. However, those talks fell through, and Tolkien returned to talks with Rayner Unwin about publishing the six *Lord of the Rings* books, reasoning that he'd rather have some of his world see print than none.

Rayner agreed, though the back-and-forth between him and Tolkien, due to Rayner's arguing for the practicalities from the perspective of a publisher, and Tolkien revising and revising his epic, took years. Eventually, Tolkien was argued down to these terms: the six books would be published as three, not simultaneously, but one after the other. And so it was that *The Lord of the Rings: The Fellowship of the Ring* hit shelves on 29 July 1954.

It was met with success. Once again C.S. Lewis went to bat publicly for his friend's work (though he joked at the time that – as by now he had begun to fall out of favour with the literary crowd, his endorsement might do more harm than good), but reviews across most publications were glowing, as they were for *The Two Towers* on 11 November 1954 and *The Return of the King* almost a year later on 20 October 1955 (this delay was caused by Tolkien's revisions, naturally).

But what was a well-received novel became a cult sensation largely for reasons outside of Tolkien and Unwin's control. In 1965, publisher Ace Books took advantage of the then-lapsed state of US copyright law to produce 'pirate' copies of *The Lord of the Rings* in America, where they were bought by American college students and, in an almost uroboric twist considering the influence of Sinclair's *Babbitt* in the hobbit ancestry, this cheaper, more accessible volumes (75c per volume) catapulted Middle-Earth and its denizens into anti-establishment and countercultural significance. The hobbits' lifestyle resonated with the hedonistic side of hippie culture, whilst the Elves and wizards connected to the polytheistic spiritualism of the movement. Many of the hallmarks of Tolkien's world, a yearning for an idealised anachronistic past, a rejection/fear of industrialisation, an embracing of the spiritual, a focus on community and the celebration of open emotional expression, were also key tenants of hippie culture. And of course, there was the central theme of defiance of unjust and cruel authoritarianism by largely non-violent people forced to defend themselves against brutality. Ironically, in trying to pen a tale of mythic quality, Tolkien had – for some of his readers – written an epic that captured the anxieties and battles of their time.

Chapter 16

A Twilight Time in the Healing Houses

So now that he had made his name, what was he to do? Unsurprisingly, as a man of simple tastes, he found fame equal parts baffling and annoying. He was touched and grateful that people responded to his work so strongly, but he was also overwhelmed by the desire to contact and talk to him personally, not least because he still firmly held that the author's life would not unlock the key to understanding his work. The number of letters he received from fans became impossible to manage alone; even after he employed a series of secretaries there was no way they could respond to everything he received. Furthermore, his address and home phone number were available from the Oxford faculty. This led to both benign annoyances, such as an overwhelming number of gifts, but also to more troubling occurrences. American fans would ring his home telephone in the small hours of the morning, disturbing both him and Edith, totally unaware of the time difference. People started to knock on his door with praise or questions, or sometimes even tried to snap a picture of the elderly professor. These harassments escalated so badly that Tolkien began to regret delaying his retirement, for not only did he no longer want for financial security but as long as he was in Oxford, people would know where to find him.

So when he eventually did retire in 1959, it was not to Oxford, but to Bournemouth. This had its advantages for Tolkien: he was finally near the sea, which he so dearly loved, but also he and Edith had been holidaying in Bournemouth, at the Miramar Hotel, for quite some time. But it was not perfect for Tolkien, the company was not to his tastes, and leaving Oxford would distancing himself from the largest concentration of his friends. However, Bournemouth was perfect for Edith. Edith had made great friends at the Miramar, which had some long-term upper-class guests: titled conservatives who enjoyed the same topics of conversation that Edith did. When she was in Bournemouth, that Oxford shyness and anxiety fell away and she chatted away with people who – given their titles, adjacent to the status symbols that had intimidated Edith in Oxford, might have intimidated her here – she spoke to as equals, holding her head high and becoming well liked on her visits. Their difference in status no longer perplexed her: her husband had written *The Lord of the Rings*! In a lot of ways, this social circle was for her very similar to her Cheltenham set from all those years ago, when she was a young adult in the Primrose League.

But just as Oxford had been impenetrable for Edith, so Bournemouth and the guests of the Miramar often left Ronald high and dry. Sometimes he enjoyed chatting with Edith's friends (and unlike he had to her, she made an effort to include him), but he missed his literary friendships, and often tired of the companionship of lords and ladies. That said, he did not resent Edith these blissful final years one little bit. As he had grown older, he perhaps realised the amount of sacrifice he had imposed on Edith to allow him to follow his dreams in Oxford, for he was adamant their retirement years were to be hers, and the burden of sacrifice was on him.

But of course, such magnanimous (or just, depending on your perspective) gestures still do cause the giver discomfort. In his diary, his private space for his depressive moods and frustrations, there are days that are nothing but complaints about the company and entertainment at the Miramar.

In general, this period of his life was humble for such a now wealthy and renowned man. He and Edith lived in a bungalow (the first centrally heated house they had ever lived in), and visited their friends at the Miramar often. They made friends with a local doctor – Dr Tolhurst – and his family. Dr Tolhurst would call round whenever they had a health complaint. When the upkeep of the house or the cooking got too much for them, they would sometimes go and stay at the Miramar overnight. This both of them enjoyed; Edith got to stay with her friends and relax, and Ronald got to enjoy plain English food with a view of the sea. Their family also visited often, which both of them loved, being the doting parents and now grandparents that they were.

But Ronald's favoured solo pursuit, which steadily took the place of his visits with his circle of male literary friends, was his writing. Both his correspondence, to which he attended regularly, and Middle-Earth. For now, Allen & Unwin were of course clamouring for *The Silmarillion*. This was Tolkien's life's work, but organising it, re-editing it, and so on and so forth, proved a gargantuan task for someone as creative as him with such a wandering mind. He began to feel overwhelmed; he wrote letters to his friends, and then letters to fans, which he would then not post because they weren't quite right, he would go looking for some papers in his ramshackle converted garage office and then he would find a new (old) note, become distracted and read through that. In a way, Tolkien had succeeded in sub-creating slightly too well; he had created a living, breathing world, with culture, and history, and had thus given himself a library for the ages made out of scribbled notes on the back of old exam papers. One can hardly blame him for getting lost in there.

But these distractions cost him time. He was the same scholar he had been as a young man, in desperate need of an E.V. Gordon, or a Simonne d'Ardenne, or even a Joe Wright or a Father Morgan to urge him to *focus*. But now those collaborators and mentors were either far away or dead, and he was stuck in his garage office with a severe writer's block. He *did* work on *The Silmarillion* in this time, but it was sporadic and slow-going. He became frustrated with himself, and spiralled into distractions, which lost him more time, leading to further frustration. He had always been a hobbyist player of patience (solitaire), but now he played more and more obsessively, coming up with multiple new strategies to share with other players.

It is easy to slide into a somewhat inaccurate view of the Tolkien of this era as a depressed man, a relic from a bygone age, two splintered and fallen friendship groups, isolated and miserable, unable to even work to soothe his solace. This would be inaccurate; he did sacrifice some of his creature comforts of many years to make Edith happy, but he also enjoyed Bournemouth, wrote to many of his friends, enjoyed being able to smoke his pipe outside without the hubbub that had dogged him in Oxford. Yes, there had been black days, as there had been during many times in his life, but they were nothing new or revolutionary. He had suffered with depression for many years, and now that he was keeping a diary once again (which was always his outlet for his darker moods) this is all the written record we have, merely because journaling was therapeutic for him. He did not leave a record of his happy days, of which there were still many.

One of his enduring habits which brought him great joy was his sense of humour. He had enjoyed taking any excuse for 'school-boyish', harmless japes for most of his life. Once in Northmoor Road he had dressed up as an 'Anglo-Saxon warrior' and startled a neighbour by chasing him. Now, he amused himself with such pranks as handing over his false teeth with his change at shops. What Edith and her high society friends thought of this is sadly unrecorded.

So it was that the Tolkiens passed their retirement in tranquillity and routine, away from the oppressive weight of celebrity and frequently visited by family and friends. That is, until the Bournemouth spell came to an abrupt and tragic end. In the middle of November 1971, Edith came down with an illness. She was taken to hospital with suspected inflamed gallstones, where she never fully recovered. On the 29 November 1971, Edith Tolkien died, aged 82.

To say that this devastated Ronald would be an understatement. In spite of their profound differences, and the rocky moments in their relationship, they were each other's soulmates and loved each other deeply. Writing to Christopher in the following weeks, it is clear he had returned to his most romantic conception of her, that of his Lúthien.

'I never called Edith Lúthien – but she was the source of the story that in time became the chief part of the Silmarillion. It was first conceived in a small woodland glade filled with hemlocks at Roos in Yorkshire (where I was for a brief time in command of an outpost of the Humber Garrison in 1917, and she was able to live with me for a while). In those days her hair was raven, her skin clear, her eyes brighter than you have seen them, and she could sing – and dance. But the story has gone crooked, & I am left, and I cannot plead before the inexorable Mandos.'[1]

This is not to say that Ronald unwilling to approach the emotional complexity of their relationship: he was. In the same letter he writes about how they rescued each other from the 'dreadful sufferings of our childhoods' as best they could, and ruminates on how that shared trauma forged a bond they never let go of for the rest of their shared days, that forced separation, war, and profound differences in interest and personality could not break.[2]

But what of Edith herself? She did not keep a diary, so we have fewer records of how she felt about her life, but what can we infer? For the opportunities lost when she left Cheltenham, when she could not pursue a career as a pianist, for the social isolation she felt in Oxford, there were innumerable achievements gained. Her illegitimate birth was something that she had been deeply ashamed of, but now it was a mere footnote in a life well led. She had been an activist in youth, a talented pianist throughout her days, married the love of her life, made many friends, provided for her cousin Jennie, run her own household, inspired parts of some of the greatest fantasy literature works of her age and raised her own family. Both she and Ronald were extremely proud of that last achievement. Both of them had been orphaned, and had either never known a stable, loving home life or had only known far too briefly. They were determined to be the family they had never had.

Tolkien would not have been the man he was, and written as he did, without the inspiration and emotional and domestic support of Edith. Fittingly, alongside her name, her tombstone is engraved with the name that her love used to inscribe her into literary canon: 'Lúthien'.

In the weeks following his wife's death Tolkien stayed with family and gathered his thoughts. He could not carry on in Bournemouth without Edith, that much he knew. The loneliness would be unbearable, and yet he did not want to impose his presence on his children. Fortunately, a solution fell into his lap. Merton College Oxford offered to make him a resident honorary professor, which would not only be a high honour, but also would come with college room and board. Tolkien gratefully accepted, and so rode with the three removal men in their pantechnicon van from Bournemouth to 21 Merton Street, early March 1972.

There he lived in the upper rooms of this college house, whilst the scout and his wife charged with his care – Mr and Mrs Carr – lived in the basement rooms. The Carrs were contractually bound to make Tolkien breakfast every day, but they were kind and generous people, to whom Tolkien quickly warmed and befriended, and so they often went far beyond their duties for him – preparing him lunch or dinner if he did not feel well enough to source it himself. More often, though, he took lunch and dinner in halls at Merton, as this was free for him. If he fancied a treat, he would potter next door to the Eastgate Hotel. He had dined there on occasion with C.S. Lewis in the 1930s, but it had become an upmarket establishment since then, and if the Tollers and Jack of the 1930s were to try their luck for a plate there now they would have been priced out. However, Tolkien was now a rich man, and able to enjoy these luxuries whenever he wanted.

So what now, rest on his laurels, write and journey from his home, to Merton, to the Eastgate and back until the end of his days? Surely not for the wandering soul that had blown this way and that over the British Isles for the better part of a century. In fact, he did travel widely in his last few years, often to receive awards or commendations. Although these flooded in from abroad also, in particular America, he did not feel he could withstand such a long trip, and contented himself with travelling around the United Kingdom. As a royalist, he was deeply honoured when he accepted and received a CBE from Queen Elizabeth II in the spring of 1972, and an honorary degree from Edinburgh in the summer of 1973, but between them was a commendation that must have been extremely close to his heart. In June 1972, he received an honorary Doctorate of Letters for his non-fiction contributions to philology (though the Public Orator – Colin Hardie, his own college chum – could not resist slipping a few references to Tolkien's fiction writing into his commendation speech).

But most important to Tolkien were his visits to his family and friends in that time. He went to Italy with Priscilla and her son Simon. He visited Christopher and his second wife Baillie often, as they lived in a village near Oxford, and ran around with his grandchildren on their lawn with such energy you wouldn't know from looking that he had lumbago. He travelled to John's parish in Leeds to stay with him for a spell, and then John drove him to Hilary's fruit farm in Evesham, where the brothers caught up with each other, and drank whisky and watched cricket on Hilary's television. As Humphrey Carpenter points out, this was the only period in their lives when the two brothers looked remotely alike; the previously stalwart Hilary and slender Ronald had both become softer and plumper in their dotage, leading to a striking resemblance between them.[3] And, of course, Tolkien caught up with two people who shaped his ideas and interests since his childhood: the only other TCBS-ite to survive the war, Christopher Wiseman, and his dear cousin, Marjorie Incledon.

Ronald was able to visit Christopher, but with Marjorie he maintained a deeply personal correspondence, going so far as to confide in her that he felt 'ornamental' to the college putting him up, and very lonely, especially after the students had gone home for the holidays, leaving him, 'all alone in a large house with only the caretaker and his wife far below in the basement'.[4]

And, of course, there was still *The Silmarillion* to attend to. Even accounting for travel, and visiting, and time to grieve, and the re-organising of the papers after moving from Bournemouth to Oxford, progress was slow-going. Although Tolkien talked of a line of longevity in his ancestors that he thought he'd inherited, in reality he seemed to expect the end to come far sooner than he'd like, and so made arrangements with his son Christopher on their frequent visits that, in the event of him dying with *The Silmarillion* unpublished, Christopher was to finish it.

Between ensuring Christopher had all the tools required to complete his masterwork, and discussions with his solicitor-cum-advisor Dick Williamson, and of course publication matters to discuss with Rayner, Tolkien seemed to be planning for a long life but preparing for a short one. However, no matter how prepared one tries to be, the ending still feels sudden.

From the end of 1972 onwards, Tolkien complained of stomach problems, including fierce indigestion. But nothing showed up on X-rays, so he was sent home with a diagnosis of dyspepsia and a restricted diet to follow, including a much-resented corollary to not drink wine.

To his credit, Tolkien stuck with the diet plan for several months, until an inter-varsity dining club feast held in Cambridge. There, temptation proved too much for him, and he feasted, and found himself feeling much better, as he explained in a thank-you letter to his host a month later. This encouraged him to relax his diet against doctor's orders, and he did seem much improved.

He was feeling so well that he decided to travel to Bournemouth to stay with the Tolhursts (the doctor and his wife whom he and Edith had frequented and befriended) to celebrate Mrs Tolhurst's birthday. He travelled down on 28 August, 1973. Mrs Tolhurst's birthday celebrations were on the Thursday, and Tolkien was feeling a little under the weather, so didn't eat much, only joining in with a little champagne. But that night, at the Tolhursts, Tolkien was in a great deal of pain, and was rushed to a private hospital first thing in the morning. He was diagnosed with an acute stomach ulcer, and it was bleeding. Those family members that could reach him in time rushed to him. Priscilla and John made it, but by horrible coincidence Christopher and Michael were on holiday in

France and Switzerland, respectively. At first, it appeared to be a false alarm, and he seemed to recover, but – in haunting similarity to the fatal infection that killed his own father during his recovery – by Saturday a chest infection had set in, and he could not fight it.

In the early morning of Sunday, 2 September, 1973, J.R.R. Tolkien died. He was 81. He was buried in the plot in Wolvercote cemetery where Edith was housed. Strikingly, it appears that he – or perhaps someone in his stead – did appeal to Mandos, and change his fate, for underneath his name is the inscription 'Beren'.

Chapter 17

Legacy, or the Sub-creations

No author's life story truly ends with their death, for there is a reason why they are remembered to the point of being worthy of a life story. And Tolkien, like most authors, is most remembered for the impact of his work.

It would be disingenuous to only discuss his fiction here, for his contributions to philology were worthy of renown in their own right. The work he did to revivify old texts, preserve and document West Midlands' dialects, and the style in which he wrote his treaties were vital contribution to philology as a whole. He inspired his students and colleagues, and breathed life into philology itself for many people.

And Middle-Earth... what a spectacular legacy to leave. Not just a book, or a series of books, but a whole world, which has delighted people in the decades following its release. The direct legacy of Middle-Earth are the numerous other properties that are set in that world. The books edited, collated and written by Christopher Tolkien in continuation of his father's noted down ideas had to be released posthumously. The two film trilogies of *The Hobbit* and *The Lord of the Rings,* adapted by Peter Jackson, Philippa Boyens and Fran Walsh, bring the majesty of Middle-Earth to a new medium with a different, more consistent tone. Elements are both lost and gained in adaption, as is the case in changing any story from one medium to another.

But there are more obscure adaptations which are worth noting, which create a balance between sincere adaption, and desperate ploy to capitalise on Tolkien's name. Of the film adaptations, there is a charming low-budget Soviet version of *The Hobbit*, broadcast in 1985. It is a television play aimed at quite young children, but is clearly made with a sincere passion and understanding of the source material. However, the first ever film adaptation was not made in the same spirit. There is a bizarre barely animated cash-grab/bastardisation hailing from America, called *The Hobbit!*, which was released in 1966 and runs to less than twelve minutes long. Among the many changes from the source material, the three trolls are two 'groans', goblins are 'grabblins', the Dwarven King Thorin Oakenshield of Erebor is a human general of Dale, and a seemingly human princess was added, whom Bilbo weds at the end. This seems to have been a project by producer William L. Snyder solely to keep the adaptation rights (which he had bought from the Tolkien estate relatively cheaply beforehand), which had become very lucrative in 1966, but that still begs the question of why they changed these details if they were trying as little as possible. A slightly improved American animated adaptation of *The Hobbit* came out of Rankin and Bass in the 1977, fashioned with a similar pseudo-medieval meets American tall-tale soundscape as Disney's *Robin Hood*, which had been released four years earlier. In this version Gandalf (voiced by veteran filmmaker John Huston) has a noticeable American accent (one wonders what Tolkien would have made of *that!*), Tolkien's song lyrics are set to 1970's American neo-folk, and Elrond is bearded, balding and has a permanent halo, making him resemble a Christian saint. It is entertaining but often unintentionally hilarious in its interpretation of Tolkien's work (due to a line about Smaug's 'cat-like' eyes, Smaug himself resembles a large long-necked cat, for example, and the goblins also have many feline qualities).

The *Lord of the Rings* was not spared its share of sometimes questionable adaptations. There was the ambitious Ralph Bakshi one, which captured some of its spirit and had some startlingly beautiful rotoscoped animation that conveys the feeling behind the works, but also a 1979 Rankin and Bass version of *The Return of the King* (just *The Return of the King*, specifically) which featured Samwise having a hallucination/fantasy sequence whilst carrying the One Ring in which – among other things – he turns an Orc into an anteater.

Interestingly, in life, Tolkien was not a devout purist to his own work when it came to the prospect of adaptation. Writing to Christopher in 1957, regarding interest from American filmmakers, he said 'Stanley [Unwin] & I have agreed on our policy: *Art or Cash*.'[1]

This is not to say that there have not been contentious moments in bringing Tolkien's work to screen; Christopher Tolkien disagreed with his son Simon Tolkien's involvement with the Jackson-Boyens-Walsh *Lord of the Rings* trilogy so severely that Simon was excluded from the board of the Tolkien Estate, and Christopher and Simon did not speak for several years (though they have since resolved their differences).[2]

The Jackson-Boyens-Walsh adaptations are perhaps the most successful sub-creations because they bring their own themes and ideas to play in Tolkien's world, not merely trying to rotely regurgitate Tolkien's work into a medium ill-suited for it, but instead adapting core concepts and exploring new ideas whilst still having a deep understanding and profound respect for Tolkien's work. That said, they, and Warner Bros' involvement with the licence, are the gateway into the Arda marred of sub-creations. The fame and appeal of Tolkien's work has made it very powerful, and powerful things in the wrong hands become dangerous things. Warner Bros allegedly intervened in laws of New Zealand, leveraging the production power of *The Hobbit* trilogy to break the New Zealand actor and crew unions by supporting the passing of The Employment Relations (Film Production Work) Amendment Bill 29 October 2010 (colloquially named the 'Hobbit law'), ushering in a new era of unsafe working conditions in the New Zealand film industry, removing the power to collectively bargain by treating all actors and crew as contractors.[3,4] At time of writing, elements of the legislation are being revised to empower New Zealand workers again, protecting the rights to collective bargaining, but in the wake of the Hobbit law, striking will be still be illegal.[5]

The marred sub-creations do not end there. On 30 June 2017, Warner Bros settled out of court for undisclosed terms with plaintiffs including the Tolkien Estate, the Tolkien Trust, HarperCollins, and Allen & Unwin, ending an $80 million lawsuit for alleged misuse of their licence by using *The Lord of the Rings* and *The Hobbit* branding for online casinos among other products. The plaintiffs argued that such products actively harmed the legacy of Tolkien's work.[6]

Ironically, the point of contention (that Warner only had licence for the *tangible* merchandising rights, as their 1969 contract was drawn prior to the existence of digital-only products and – unfortunately – online casinos),[7] and Warner's ability to push and test its limits has led to some of the most creative and innovative sub-creations in the video game industry.

There have been many video games set in Middle-Earth, some where you play as a main character going through the events of the story, such as *The Hobbit* game released in 2003 (which has since become 'abandonware'), and other games that simply take place in the world of Middle-Earth, such as the *Shadow of Mordor* games, and *The Lord of the Rings: War In The North*, which takes a trio of original characters and pits them in the Northern Front of the events concurrent to *The Lord of the Rings*. All of the above efforts have their own charm and interesting ideas, small fragments of world building extrapolated from half-forgotten footnotes or a deep understanding of the core texts. But again, this is a fallen Earth. The October after Warner Bros reached a settlement with regards to their treatment of the Middle-Earth licence, they released the sequel to *Shadow of Mordor*, *Shadow of War*, which contained a sizeable number of microtransactions (a purchasing system in some video games, which cost real money and typically constantly advertise themselves to players, therefore disrupting the flow of the other core parts of the game in ways to designed to make players want to buy them to progress and/or have the best experience).

But aside from licensed works, there are of course the fan-works which Tolkien inspired. Middle-Earth being as complex as it is, thousands upon thousands of dedicated fans have drawn their own interpretations of the characters, written new poems and stories in that world, redrawn the maps, etc. Tolkien's own treatment of his fantasy land as a living world inspired others to do the same, and communities who study (and in some cases even speak) the languages he created thrive across the world. Perhaps one of the most interesting and pervasive elements of this global community of fan artists and fan fiction writers are the LGBTQIA fans who read queerness into Tolkien's portrayal of strong male friendships, usually as homosexuality and/or asexuality. This was of course not Tolkien's intention, but the nature of his world leads LGBTQIA fans to identify strongly with his characters. As Anna Smol wrote in her paper on the subject, Tolkien's writing, despite being extremely chaste, 'has always elicited strong reactions focusing on sex'.[8] Additionally, Tolkien's centring of pining and emotional and physical openness inspired generations of people, marginalised for their sexualities, to see their experiences reflected in the heroes of Middle-Earth. This is, of course, not the same as genuine representation, but is perhaps a reason why many LGBTQIA fans have a special place for Middle-Earth in their hearts, as well as a strong defiance of attempts to override queer interpretations of the stories through adaptation.[9]

But sub-creations must always have a mind of their own, a spark of creativity not derived from their original, which is why it could be argued that Middle-Earth's successors are the not adaptions of its own stories and world, but the countless original stories it created. Western fantasy, in particular pseudo-Medieval fantasy, is heavily derived from Tolkien, usually intermingled with Greek myths and (more recently) the world of Lovecraft too. Perhaps the most famous example of this is the tabletop role-playing game (TTRPG) *Dungeons & Dragons*, which has what became the royalty-free name for hobbit-like creatures, 'halflings', as one of the species that not only live in the world, but that the player characters can be. In fact, Tolkien's vision of fantasy became so widespread and popularised in the last few decades that it has spawned the genre and word 'Tolkienesque' fantasy, as well as its less fortunate and oxymoronic cousin 'standard fantasy'.

For its true that what was once Tolkien's 'private nonsense' has now become ubiquitous. Mention a Western fantasy to anyone and they can immediately pinpoint certain archetypes of the genre that were modernised by Tolkien: his version of Elves, hobbit-like creatures, and Dwarves. Orcs too, although the word existed prior to Tolkien to describe a type of demon, because of Tolkien's influence it has come to mean a new creature, somewhere between a goblin and a troll. Also, in a twist of fate that would have probably delighted Tolkien, the invention of working languages for fictional worlds became not only the private project of many a fantasy writer, but also another genre-wide popular archetype.

Of course, this popularity is not without its drawbacks. Aside from questionable uses of the Middle-Earth licence, there is the burnout factor. So many elements of Tolkien's work are reproduced over and over, sometimes gaining a new context but often becoming more and more removed from their original meaning that now audiences are fatigued. Additionally, there is the overemphasis of his influence. People call Tolkien the father of modern fantasy, and attribute almost anything in the fantasy genre as finding its roots in his work, when this is simply not true. Tolkien is a crucial, genre-defining figure in *Western* fantasy, specifically the Anglo-centric and American chapters of this genre; almost every other culture has its own fantasy fiction genres and standout historical figures who popularised certain archetypes. Being a fantasy writer should not mean being beholden to having your inspirations mis-attributed to Tolkien due to a lack of knowledge on the part of the Western audience when their work reaches it. Fantasy fiction for adults is being written by people all over the world, from every background and culture, Indigenous and diaspora alike. It disrespects both them and the actual impressive achievements of Tolkien's lifetime to overextend the reality of what he did and who he reached.

In England, America, and New Zealand in particular, his work did reach large audiences. And although he joked in later life that he had given up on what had been his dream of creating a mythology for England, it could be argued that he succeeded. One need only look at the prominence of imagery of the Shire in Danny Boyle's London 2012 Olympics opening ceremony to see that the world Tolkien created is considered a piece of English cultural heritage of mythic importance.

It should not be overlooked that many people who write fantasy do so in defiance of Tolkien. Tolkien poured his heart and soul into his world, and although many of the themes of his tales are universal, who will be good, or evil, or right or wrong align with his political views and beliefs, and not everyone is going to agree with those politics. There is almost a sub-genre of Tolkienesque fiction that takes the familiar settings, and aims to deconstruct some of the troubling implications of them, or to tell a similar story from a different perspective.

And this isn't a bad thing. This is not Morgoth introducing chaos into the Music of the Ainur, this is all the pagan gods adding their notes to the music, building fuller worlds. Tolkien's Middle-Earth is so beloved precisely because it is open to interpretation and commentary. There is nothing quite like Middle-Earth, but that is alright. Worlds created in defiance or homage to it have their own unique elements to them. Stories created in Middle-Earth each have their own distinct flavour. Nothing will ever be J.R.R. Tolkien's Middle-Earth again, because that was singular, but Middle-Earth itself is enduring. No character Tolkien writes from the perspective of is omniscient or perfect. No-one has a full unbiased view of their own history. So we experience Middle-Earth through its storytellers: through Bilbo, Frodo, Samwise and even the Elven scholars, and we go on to tell our own stories with our own crafted storytellers, or retell the stories of Middle-Earth in our own way. Middle-Earth is made richer by Christopher Tolkien writing and releasing new histories; by Jackson, Boyens and Walsh bringing their broader perspective to life onscreen; by Bakshi's singular imagery, and by bedroom scholars pouring over Quenyan, or Sindarin, or even Orkish.

Gajum mir, Arnhai Tolkien.
(Sleep well, Mr Tolkien.)

Appendix

A Note on Chapter 11

(Author's Note: the following paragraphs discuss allegations of child sexual abuse. Given that this is a topic that carries a huge amount of trauma for many, I thought it appropriate to place a warning here.)

Anote to include about the dynamic of the Tolkien household. It has become public record that the large number of male academics who visited and stayed overnight at the Tolkien house allegedly put at least one of Tolkien's children at risk of abuse. John, the eldest, was recorded in 1994 alleging he was sexually abused as a child by one of Tolkien's friends. In the recording, he describes an academic who would often sleep in his bed (he does not name who), and one night when this happened, John woke up without his pyjamas on, though he had gone to sleep wearing them.[1] This recording was made by a man named Christopher Carrie, who alleged that John abused him in his childhood twice. Carrie is one of at least three alleged victims of childhood sexual abuse by John, during his years as a priest in the 1950s and 60s with ties to schools and scout groups in Birmingham and Stoke-on-Trent, the Independent Inquiry Child Sexual Abuse (IICSA) heard.[2]

These allegations cast a pall over the Tolkien household. If these events happened as described, then Tolkien's heedless enthusiasm for the company of male intellectuals may have cost his family and others dearly, potentially casting a decades-long shadow. This is not to blame Ronald Tolkien for the alleged actions of his male friend or his son in adulthood, but to fully contextualise Tolkien's life, even aspects that may have been disturbing or even traumatising.

Notes

Introduction

1. Harrod, H, *How Tolkien became the man who made Middle-earth* (The Financial Times, 4 May 2018): https://www.ft.com/content/
2. Duriez, C., *Tolkien: The Making of a Legend* (Lion Hudson plc, 2012, 1st Edition): p.193
3. Carpenter, H., *J.R.R. Tolkien, A Biography* (HarperCollins Publishers, 2002, 8th Edition): p.171

Chapter One

1. Carpenter, H., *J.R.R. Tolkien, A Biography* (HarperCollins Publishers, 2002, 8th Edition): p.22
2. Carpenter, H., *J.R.R. Tolkien, A Biography* (HarperCollins Publishers, 2002, 8th Edition): p.23
3. Carpenter, H., *J.R.R. Tolkien, A Biography* (HarperCollins Publishers, 2002, 8th Edition): pp.23-4
4. Carpenter, H., *J.R.R. Tolkien, A Biography* (HarperCollins Publishers, 2002, 8th Edition): p.25
5. Tolkien, J.R.R., *The Lord of the Rings* (HarperCollins Publishers, 2007, 50th Anniversary Omnibus Edition): p.1133
6. Duriez, C., *Tolkien: The Making of a Legend* (Lion Hudson plc, 2012, 1st Edition): p.11
7. Tolkien, J.R.R., *The Letters of J.R.R. Tolkien*, edited by Humphrey Carpenter (HarperCollins Publishers, 2006, 8th Edition, Letter 163): p.217
8. Tolkien, J.R.R., *The Silmarillion* (HarperCollins Publishers, 2013, 1st Edition): p.77
9. Carpenter, H., *J.R.R. Tolkien, A Biography* (HarperCollins Publishers, 2002, 8th Edition): p.27
10. Carpenter, H., *J.R.R. Tolkien, A Biography* (HarperCollins Publishers, 2002, 8th Edition): p.29
11. Tolkien, J.R.R., BBC Radio interview with Denys Gueroult, *Now Read On*, 16 December 1970
12. Duriez, C., *Tolkien: The Making of a Legend* (Lion Hudson plc, 2012, 1st Edition): p.14
13. Carpenter, H., *J.R.R. Tolkien, A Biography* (HarperCollins Publishers, 2002, 8th Edition): pp.30-1

Chapter Two

1. Measuring Worth 'real price' calculation: https://www.measuringworth.com/calculators/ukcompare/relativevalue.php

2. Carpenter, H., *J.R.R. Tolkien, A Biography* (HarperCollins Publishers, 2002, 8th Edition): p.33

3. Carpenter, H., *J.R.R. Tolkien, A Biography* (HarperCollins Publishers, 2002, 8th Edition): p.34

4. Carpenter, H., *J.R.R. Tolkien, A Biography* (HarperCollins Publishers, 2002, 8th Edition): p.35

5. *Ibid.*

6. Tolkien, J. & Tolkien, P., *The Tolkien Family Album* (HarperCollins Publishers, 1992 1st Edition): p.21

7. Carpenter, H., *J.R.R. Tolkien, A Biography* (HarperCollins Publishers, 2002, 8th Edition): p.37

8. Ezard, J., *JRR Tolkien Interview* (The Guardian, 28 December 1991)

9. Carpenter, H., *J.R.R. Tolkien, A Biography* (HarperCollins Publishers, 2002, 8th Edition): p.36

10. Ezard, J., *JRR Tolkien Interview* (The Guardian, 28 December 1991)

11. Duriez, C., *Tolkien: The Making of a Legend* (Lion Hudson plc, 2012, 1st Edition): p.15

12. Carpenter, H., *J.R.R. Tolkien, A Biography* (HarperCollins Publishers, 2002, 8th Edition): p.39

13. Carpenter, H., *J.R.R. Tolkien, A Biography* (HarperCollins Publishers, 2002, 8th Edition): p.37

14. Tolkien, J.R.R., *On Fairy-Stories (The Monsters and the Critics)* (HarperCollins Publishers, 2012, Ebook Edition): loc 2252

15. Carpenter, H., *J.R.R. Tolkien, A Biography* (HarperCollins Publishers, 2002, 8th Edition): p.39

16. Carpenter, H., *J.R.R. Tolkien, A Biography* (HarperCollins Publishers, 2002, 8th Edition): p.40

17. Duriez, C., *Tolkien: The Making of a Legend* (Lion Hudson plc, 2012, 1st Edition): p.16

18. Tolkien, J.R.R., *The Letters of J.R.R. Tolkien*, edited by Humphrey Carpenter (HarperCollins Publishers, 2006, 8th Edition, Letter 153): p.187

19. Tolkien, J.R.R., *The Letters of J.R.R. Tolkien*, edited by Humphrey Carpenter (HarperCollins Publishers, 2006, 8th Edition, Letter 153): pp.188-9

20. *Ibid.*

21. Tolkien, J.R.R., *The Letters of J.R.R. Tolkien*, edited by Humphrey Carpenter (HarperCollins Publishers, 2006, 8th Edition, Letter 340): p.421

22. Measuring Worth 'real price' calculation: https://www.measuringworth.com/calculators/ukcompare/relativevalue.php

23. Carpenter, H., *J.R.R. Tolkien, A Biography* (HarperCollins Publishers, 2002, 8th Edition): p.42

Chapter Three

1. Duriez, C., *Tolkien: The Making of a Legend* (Lion Hudson plc, 2012, 1st Edition): p.18

2. Carpenter, H., *J.R.R. Tolkien, A Biography* (HarperCollins Publishers, 2002, 8th Edition): p.45

3. Tolkien, J.R.R., *The Letters of J.R.R. Tolkien*, edited by Humphrey Carpenter (HarperCollins Publishers, 2006, 8th Edition, Letter 163): p212

4. Carpenter, H., *J.R.R. Tolkien, A Biography* (HarperCollins Publishers, 2002, 8th Edition): p.46
5. Duriez, C., *Tolkien: The Making of a Legend* (Lion Hudson plc, 2012, 1st Edition): p.70
6. Carpenter, H., *J.R.R. Tolkien, A Biography* (HarperCollins Publishers, 2002, 8th Edition): p.47
7. Carpenter, H., *J.R.R. Tolkien, A Biography* (HarperCollins Publishers, 2002, 8th Edition): p.45
8. Carpenter, H., *J.R.R. Tolkien, A Biography* (HarperCollins Publishers, 2002, 8th Edition): pp.46-7
9. *Ibid.*
10. Carpenter, H., *J.R.R. Tolkien, A Biography* (HarperCollins Publishers, 2002, 8th Edition): p.47
11. Carpenter, H., *J.R.R. Tolkien, A Biography* (HarperCollins Publishers, 2002, 8th Edition): pp.48-9
12. Duriez, C., *Tolkien: The Making of a Legend* (Lion Hudson plc, 2012, 1st Edition): p.21
13. Tolkien, J.R.R., *The Letters of J.R.R. Tolkien*, edited by Humphrey Carpenter (HarperCollins Publishers, 2006, 8th Edition, Letter 250): p.340
14. Tolkien, J.R.R., *The Letters of J.R.R. Tolkien*, edited by Humphrey Carpenter (HarperCollins Publishers, 2006, 8th Edition, Letter 266): pp.353-4
15. Duriez, C., *Tolkien: The Making of a Legend* (Lion Hudson plc, 2012, 1st Edition): p.22
16. *Ibid.*

Chapter Four

1. Carpenter, H., *J.R.R. Tolkien, A Biography* (HarperCollins Publishers, 2002, 8th Edition): p.51
2. Carpenter, H., *J.R.R. Tolkien, A Biography* (HarperCollins Publishers, 2002, 8th Edition): pp.50-1
3. Carpenter, H., *J.R.R. Tolkien, A Biography* (HarperCollins Publishers, 2002, 8th Edition): p.56
4. Carpenter, H., *J.R.R. Tolkien, A Biography* (HarperCollins Publishers, 2002, 8th Edition): p.57
5. Duriez, C., *Tolkien: The Making of a Legend* (Lion Hudson plc, 2012, 1st Edition): p.41
6. Duriez, C., *Tolkien: The Making of a Legend* (Lion Hudson plc, 2012, 1st Edition): p.39
7. Duriez, C., *Tolkien: The Making of a Legend* (Lion Hudson plc, 2012, 1st Edition): p.40
8. Carpenter, H., *J.R.R. Tolkien, A Biography* (HarperCollins Publishers, 2002, 8th Edition): p.69
9. Duriez, C., *Tolkien: The Making of a Legend* (Lion Hudson plc, 2012, 1st Edition): p.48
10. *King Edward's School Chronicle* (Vol. XXVII, March 1912): No. 191
11. Carpenter, H., *J.R.R. Tolkien, A Biography* (HarperCollins Publishers, 2002, 8th Edition): p.59

Chapter Five
1. Carpenter, H., *J.R.R. Tolkien, A Biography* (HarperCollins Publishers, 2002, 8th Edition): p.61
2. Carpenter, H., *J.R.R. Tolkien, A Biography* (HarperCollins Publishers, 2002, 8th Edition): p.62
3. Carpenter, H., *J.R.R. Tolkien, A Biography* (HarperCollins Publishers, 2002, 8th Edition): p.21
4. Carpenter, H., *J.R.R. Tolkien, A Biography* (HarperCollins Publishers, 2002, 8th Edition): pp. 64–5
5. Carpenter, H., *J.R.R. Tolkien, A Biography* (HarperCollins Publishers, 2002, 8th Edition): p.65
6. Carpenter, H., *J.R.R. Tolkien, A Biography* (HarperCollins Publishers, 2002, 8th Edition): p.66
7. *Ibid.*
8. *Ibid.*

Chapter Six
1. Tolkien, J.R.R., *The Letters of J.R.R. Tolkien*, edited by Humphrey Carpenter (HarperCollins Publishers, 2006, 8th Edition, Letter 306): p.392
2. Cooke, A., *'Founders of the Primrose League (act. 1883–c.1918)'*, *Oxford Dictionary of National Biography* (Oxford University Press, September 2014, Online Edition)
3. Carpenter, H., *J.R.R. Tolkien, A Biography* (HarperCollins Publishers, 2002, 8th Edition): p.67
4. Carpenter, H., *J.R.R. Tolkien, A Biography* (HarperCollins Publishers, 2002, 8th Edition): p.80
5. Sladen, C., *Idle Scholar Who Brought Local Language to Book* (Oxford Today 22, no. 3, Trinity 2010)
6. Tolkien, J.R.R., *The Letters of JRR Tolkien*, edited by Humphrey Carpenter (HarperCollins Publishers, 2006, 8th Edition, Letter 250): p.336
7. Carpenter, H., *J.R.R. Tolkien, A Biography* (HarperCollins Publishers, 2002, 8th Edition): p83

Chapter Seven
1. Carpenter, H., *J.R.R. Tolkien, A Biography* (HarperCollins Publishers, 2002, 8th Edition): p. 87
2. Duriez, C., *Tolkien: The Making of a Legend* (Lion Hudson plc, 2012, 1st Edition): p.62
3. Carpenter, H., *J.R.R. Tolkien, A Biography* (HarperCollins Publishers, 2002, 8th Edition): p.89
4. Carpenter, H., *J.R.R. Tolkien, A Biography* (HarperCollins Publishers, 2002, 8th Edition): p.94

Chapter Eight
1. Carpenter, H., *J.R.R. Tolkien, A Biography* (HarperCollins Publishers, 2002, 8th Edition) p.104
2. Carpenter, H., *J.R.R. Tolkien, A Biography* (HarperCollins Publishers, 2002, 8th Edition) p.105
3. Crist of Cynewulf (Lines 104 to 108): https://glaemscrafu.jrrvf.com/english/crist.html

4. *King Edward's School Chronicle* (Vol. XXVII, March 1911): pp.22-27
5. Garth, J., *Tolkien and the Great War: The Threshold of Middle-earth* (HarperCollins Publishers, 2004, 4th Edition): p.92
6. Garth, J., *Tolkien and the Great War: The Threshold of Middle-earth* (HarperCollins Publishers, 2004, 4th Edition): pp.115-16
7. Garth, J., *Tolkien and the Great War: The Threshold of Middle-earth* (HarperCollins Publishers, 2004, 4th Edition): pp.117-18
8. Morgan, CL, Captain, *Letter to Robert Cary Gilson*, 12 July 1916.
9. Garth, J., *Tolkien and the Great War: The Threshold of Middle-earth* (HarperCollins Publishers, 2004, 4th Edition): p.176
10. Garth, J., *Tolkien and the Great War: The Threshold of Middle-earth* (HarperCollins Publishers, 2004, 4th Edition): p.211
11. Garth, J., *Tolkien and the Great War: The Threshold of Middle-earth* (HarperCollins Publishers, 2004, 4th Edition): p.212

Chapter Nine
1. Tolkien, J.R.R., *The Letters of J.R.R. Tolkien*, edited by Humphrey Carpenter (HarperCollins Publishers, 2006, 8th Edition, Letter 45): p.54
2. Carpenter, H., *J.R.R. Tolkien, A Biography* (HarperCollins Publishers, 2002, 8th Edition): pp.77-8
3. Tolkien, J.R.R., *The Letters of J.R.R. Tolkien*, edited by Humphrey Carpenter (HarperCollins Publishers, 2006, 8th Edition, Letter 45): pp.48-54
4. *Ibid.*
5. *Ibid.*
6. Tolkien, J.R.R., *The Letters of J.R.R. Tolkien*, edited by Humphrey Carpenter (HarperCollins Publishers, 2006, 8th . Edition, Letter 52): p.64
7. Tolkien, J.R.R., *The Letters of J.R.R. Tolkien*, edited by Humphrey Carpenter (HarperCollins Publishers, 2006, 8th Edition, Letter 45): p.54
8. Garth, J., *Tolkien and the Great War: The Threshold of Middle-earth* (HarperCollins Publishers, 2004, 4th Edition): p125
9. Tolkien, J.R.R., *The Letters of J.R.R. Tolkien*, edited by Humphrey Carpenter (HarperCollins Publishers, 2006, 8th Edition, Letter 226) p.303.
10. Tolkien, J.R.R., *'Foreword to the Second Edition', The Lord of the Rings* (HarperCollins Publishers, 2007 50th Anniversary Omnibus Edition): p.xxiv.

Chapter Ten
1. Carpenter, H., *J.R.R. Tolkien, A Biography* (HarperCollins Publishers, 2002, 8th Edition): p.126
2. Carpenter, H., *J.R.R. Tolkien, A Biography* (HarperCollins Publishers, 2002, 8th Edition): p.137
3. Carpenter, H., *J.R.R. Tolkien, A Biography* (HarperCollins Publishers, 2002, 8th Edition): p.141
4. *Ibid.*
5. Carpenter, H., *J.R.R. Tolkien, A Biography* (HarperCollins Publishers, 2002, 8th Edition): p.142
6. White, M., *Tolkien, A Biography* (Little, Brown And Company, 2001): p.106
7. White, M., *Tolkien, A Biography* (Little, Brown And Company, 2001): p.108

Chapter Eleven

1. Swanton, M., *Beowulf, Revised Edition* (Manchester University Press, 1997, 5th Edition):p.35
2. Carpenter, H., *J.R.R. Tolkien, A Biography* (HarperCollins Publishers, 2002, 8th Edition): p.180
3. Swanton, M., *Beowulf, Revised Edition* (Manchester University Press, 1997, 5th Edition): p.2
4. Carpenter, H., *J.R.R. Tolkien, A Biography* (HarperCollins Publishers, 2002, 8th Edition): p.192
5. Tolkien, J.R.R., *The Letters of J.R.R. Tolkien*, edited by Humphrey Carpenter (HarperCollins Publishers, 2006, 8th Edition, Letter 332): p.416

Chapter Twelve

1. Carpenter, H., *J.R.R. Tolkien, A Biography* (HarperCollins Publishers, 2002, 8th Edition): p.220
2. Anonymous, *History, Founding Fellows, M. Elaine Griffiths (1909 – 1996)* (St Anne's College, University of Oxford): https://www.st-annes.ox.ac.uk/this-is-st-annes/history/founding-fellows/m-elaine-griffiths/
3. Tolkien, J.R.R., *The Letters of J.R.R. Tolkien*, edited by Humphrey Carpenter (HarperCollins Publishers, 2006, 8th Edition, Letter 10): p.15
4. Bratman, D., *Ten miscellanies make a blog post* (Livejounal, 5 November 2013): https://kalimac.livejournal.com/694167.html
5. Burrow, T., *CS Lewis supported secret heritage gang* (Oxford Mail, 13 October 2013): https://www.oxfordmail.co.uk/news/10737947.cs-lewis-supported-secret-heritage-gang/
6. Anderson, D.A., Tolkien, J.R.R., *The Annotated Hobbit: The Hobbit, or There and Back Again* (Houghton Mifflin Harcourt, 1988): p.104, p.176, pp.325-27

Chapter Thirteen

1. Garth, J., *Tolkien and the Great War: The Threshold of Middle-earth* (HarperCollins Publishers, 2004, 4th Edition): p.190
2. Tolkien, J.R.R., *The Letters of J.R.R. Tolkien*, edited by Humphrey Carpenter (HarperCollins Publishers, 2006, 8th Edition, Letter 35): p.42
3. Tolkien, J.R.R., *The Letters of J.R.R. Tolkien*, edited by Humphrey Carpenter (HarperCollins Publishers, 2006, 8th Edition, Carpenter's footnote to Letter 35): p.436
4. Stenström, A, *Mythopoic Society Yahoo Group discussion*, 20 September 2009 https://groups.yahoo.com/neo/groups/mythsoc/conversations/messages/20852
5. Anonymous Historian, '*JRR Tolkien trained as British spy*', Telegraph, 16 September 2009: Author uncredited: https://www.telegraph.co.uk/news/uknews/6197169/JRR-Tolkien-trained-as-British-spy.html
6. Smith, N., *The Wisdom of the Shire: A Short Guide to a Long and Happy Life*, (Hachette UK: 2012): p78
7. Brennan, D., *THE HOBBIT: HOW TOLKIEN SUNK A GERMAN ANTI-SEMITIC INQUIRY INTO HIS RACE* (Newsweek, 21 September 2018): https://www.newsweek.com/hobbit-how-tolkien-sunk-german-anti-semitic-inquiry-his-race-1132744

8. Tolkien, J.R.R., *The Letters of J.R.R. Tolkien*, edited by Humphrey Carpenter (HarperCollins Publishers, 2006, 8th Edition, Letter 30): p.37

9. *Ibid.*

10. Starr, J.S.K., *Academic Correspondence*, (WhatsApp 22 March 2020): cached

Chapter Fourteen

1. Garth, J., *Tolkien and the Great War: The Threshold of Middle-earth* (HarperCollins Publishers, 2004, 4th Edition): p.277

2. Chance, J., *Tolkien, Self and Other: 'This Queer Creature'* (The New Middle Ages, Palgrave Macmillan, 2016)

Chapter Fifteen

1. Tolkien, J.R.R., *The Letters of J.R.R. Tolkien*, edited by Humphrey Carpenter (HarperCollins Publishers, 2006, 8th Edition, Letter 17): p.24

2. Unwin, S., *The Truth About A Publisher* (George Allen & Unwin, 1960): p.301

Chapter Sixteen

1. Tolkien, J.R.R., *The Letters of J.R.R. Tolkien*, edited by Humphrey Carpenter (HarperCollins Publishers, 2006, 8th Edition, Letter 340): p.420

2. Tolkien, J.R.R., *The Letters of J.R.R. Tolkien*, edited by Humphrey Carpenter (HarperCollins Publishers, 2006, 8th Edition, Letter 340): p.421

3. Carpenter, H., *J.R.R. Tolkien, A Biography* (HarperCollins Publishers, 2002, 8th Edition): p.337

4. Tolkien, J.R.R., *The Letters of J.R.R. Tolkien*, edited by Humphrey Carpenter (HarperCollins Publishers, 2006, 8th Edition, Letter 341): p.421

Chapter Seventeen

1. Tolkien, J.R.R., *The Letters of J.R.R. Tolkien*, edited by Humphrey Carpenter (HarperCollins Publishers, 2006, 8th Edition, Letter 202): p.261

2. Hastings, C., *JRR Tolkien's grandson 'cut off from literary inheritance'* (The Telegraph, 24 February 2003): https://www.telegraph.co.uk/news/uknews/1422943/J-R-R-Tolkiens-grandson-cut-off-from-literary-inheritance.html

3. Nixon, K.K., *Hobbit law repeal: How did we get here?* (Stuff, 31 October 2017): https://www.stuff.co.nz/entertainment/film/98414573/hobbit-law-repeal-how-did-we-get-here

4. Anonymous, *Hobbit legislation passed in New Zealand* (BBC News Asia-Pacific, 29 October 2010): https://www.bbc.co.uk/news/world-asia-pacific-11649734

5. Cheng, D., *Hobbit law stays: Minimum standards coming for film industry, but striking will be illegal* (NZ Herald, 13 June 2019): https://www.nzherald.co.nz/nz/news/article.

6. Sanchez, R, *JRR Tolkien's daughter sues producers of The Hobbit* (The Telegraph, 20 November 2012): https://www.telegraph.co.uk/news/worldnews/9691966/JRR-Tolkiens-daughter-sues-producers-of-The-Hobbit.html

7. Anonymous, *Tolkien's estate settles lawsuit over online gambling link to author's books* (The Straits Times, 4 July 2017): https://www.straitstimes.com/lifestyle/entertainment/tolkiens-estate-settles-lawsuit-over-online-gambling-link-to-authors-books

8. Smol, A., *'Oh ... Oh ... Frodo!': Readings of Male Intimacy in The Lord Of The Rings* (Modern Fiction Studies, John Hopkins University Press, Volume 50, Number 4, Winter 2004): pp. 949-79

9. Rohy, V., *Cinema, Sexuality, Mechanical Reproduction, in Tolkien and Alterity*, edited by Vaccaro, C & Kisor, Y., (The New Middle Ages, Palgrave Macmillan, 2017)

Appendix
1. Pepinster, C., *JRR Tolkien's son 'sexually abused by one of father's friends'* (The Guardian, 28 April 2019): https://www.theguardian.com/books/2019/apr/28/jrr-tolkiens-son-claims-sexually-abuse-fathers-friend
2. IICSA, *IICSA Roman Catholic Church (Birmingham) hearings transcript* (IICSA, 13 December 2018): pp.46-63 https://www.iicsa.org.uk/key-documents/8620/view/special-sitting-transcript-13-december-2018.pdf

Bibliography

Anderson, D.A., Tolkien, J.R.R., *The Annotated Hobbit: The Hobbit, or There and Back Again* (Houghton Mifflin Harcourt, 1988)

Anonymous, *King Edward's School Chronicle* (Vol. XXVII, 1 March 1912, No. 191)

Anonymous Historian, *J.R.R. Tolkien trained as British spy* (*The Telegraph*, 16 September 2009: Author uncredited): https://www.telegraph.co.uk/news/uknews/6197169/JRR-Tolkien-trained-as-British-spy.html

Anonymous, *History, Founding Fellows, M. Elaine Griffiths (1909–1996)* (St Anne's College, University of Oxford): https://www.st-annes.ox.ac.uk/this-is-st-annes/history/founding-fellows/m-elaine-griffiths/

Anonymous, *Hobbit legislation passed in New Zealand* (BBC News Asia-Pacific, 29 October 2010): https://www.bbc.co.uk/news/world-asia-pacific-11649734

Anonymous, *Tolkien's estate settles lawsuit over online gambling link to author's books* (*The Straits Times*, 4 July 2017): https://www.straitstimes.com/lifestyle/entertainment/tolkiens-estate-settles-lawsuit-over-online-gambling-link-to-authors-books

Bratman, D., *Ten miscellanies make a blog post* (Livejournal, 5 November 2013): https://kalimac.livejournal.com/694167.html

Brennan, D., *The Hobbit: How Tolkien sunk a German Anti-Semitic inquiry about his race* (*Newsweek*, 21 September 2018): https://www.newsweek.com/hobbit-how-tolkien-sunk-german-anti-semitic-inquiry-his-race-1132744

Burrow, T., *C.S. Lewis supported secret heritage gang* (*Oxford Mail*, 13 October 2013): https://www.oxfordmail.co.uk/news/10737947.cs-lewis-supported-secret-heritage-gang/

Carpenter, H., *J.R.R. Tolkien, A Biography* (HarperCollins Publishers, 2002, 8th Edition)

Chance, J., *Tolkien, Self and Other: 'This Queer Creature'* (The New Middle Ages, Palgrave Macmillan, 2016)

Cheng, D., *Hobbit law stays: Minimum standards coming for film industry, but striking will be illegal* (*NZ Herald*, 13 June 2019): https://www.nzherald.co.nz/nz/news/article.cfm?c_id=1&objectid=12240140

Cooke, A., *'Founders of the Primrose League (act. 1883–c.1918)', Oxford Dictionary of National Biography* (Oxford University Press, September 2014, Online Edition)

Crist of Cynewulf (Lines 104 to 108): https://glaemscrafu.jrrvf.com/english/crist.html

Duriez, C., *Tolkien: The Making of a Legend* (Lion Hudson plc, 2012, 1st Edition)

Ezard, J., *J.R.R. Tolkien Article* (*The Guardian*, 28 December 1991)

Garth, J., *Tolkien and the Great War: The Threshold of Middle-earth* (HarperCollins Publishers, 2004, 4th Edition)

Hammond, W.G. & Scull, C., *The J.R.R. Tolkien Companion and Guide Chronology* (Houghton Mifflin Company, 2006)

Harrod, H., *How Tolkien became the man who made Middle-earth* (*The Financial Times*, 4 May 2018): https://www.ft.com/content/c7ec7e70-4d98-11e8-97e4-13afc22d86d4

Hastings, C., *JRR Tolkien's grandson 'cut off from literary inheritance'* (*The Telegraph*, 24 February 2003): https://www.telegraph.co.uk/news/uknews/1422943/J-R-R-Tolkiens-grandson-cut-off-from-literary-inheritance.html

IICSA, *IICSA Roman Catholic Church (Birmingham) hearings transcript* (IICSA, 13 December 2018):p46-63 https://www.iicsa.org.uk/key-documents/8620/view/special-sitting-transcript-13-december-2018.pdf

Nixon, K.K., *Hobbit law repeal: How did we get here?* (*Stuff*, 31 October 2017): https://www.stuff.co.nz/entertainment/film/98414573/hobbit-law-repeal-how-did-we-get-here

Pepinster, C., *JRR Tolkien's son 'sexually abused by one of father's friends'* (*The Guardian*, 28 April 2019): https://www.theguardian.com/books/2019/apr/28/jrr-tolkiens-son-claims-sexually-abuse-fathers-friend

Rohy, V., *Cinema, Sexuality, Mechanical Reproduction, in Tolkien and Alterity*, edited by Vaccaro, C & Kisor, Y (The New Middle Ages, Palgrave Macmillan, 2017)

Sanchez, R., *JRR Tolkien's daughter sues producers of The Hobbit* (*The Telegraph*, 20 November 2012): https://www.telegraph.co.uk/news/worldnews/9691966/JRR-Tolkiens-daughter-sues-producers-of-The-Hobbit.html

Sladen, C., *Idle Scholar Who Brought Local Language to Book* (*Oxford Today*, 22 Trinity 2010, no. 3)

Smith, N., *The Wisdom of the Shire: A Short Guide to a Long and Happy Life* (Hachette UK, 2012)

Smol, A., *'Oh ... Oh ... Frodo!': Readings of Male Intimacy in The Lord Of The Rings* (Modern Fiction Studies, John Hopkins University Press, Volume 50, Number 4, Winter 2004)

Stenström, A., *Mythopaic Society Yahoo Group discussion* (20 September 2009): https://groups.yahoo.com/neo/groups/mythsoc/conversations/messages/20852?guccounter=1&guce_referrer=aHR0cHM6Ly9lbi53aWtpcGVka WEub3JnLw&guce_referrer_sig=AQAAABbojZ1jNfNKoaKntC1XSBb RWqfXVVCfevp7o8o10lkOxCMszcqEY52_We1WEOqSaTnHjW -1wqL9WEUgoMiQCq7_hbFij5xb_5QZ_omgbt7HXJjghyru0NhyPHkLY d-PJhtQo7QBdUWYCztuooMVAp9m9IQ4nWo12xS-PcUl4DUR

Swanton, M., *Beowulf – Revised Edition* (Manchester University Press, 1997, 5th Edition)

Tolkien, J.R.R., *The Hobbit* (HarperCollins Publishers, 2011, 5th Edition)

Tolkien, J.R.R., *The Lord of the Rings* (HarperCollins Publishers, 2007, Omnibus Edition)

Tolkien, J.R.R., *The Silmarillion* (HarperCollins Publishers, 2013, 1st Edition)

Tolkien, J.R.R., *On Fairy-Stories (The Monsters and the Critics)* (HarperCollins Publishers, 2012, Ebook Edition)

Tolkien, J.R.R., *The Letters of J.R.R. Tolkien, edited by Humphrey Carpenter* (HarperCollins Publishers, 2006, 8th Edition)

Tolkien, J. & P. *The Tolkien Family Album* (HarperCollins Publishers, 1992, 1st Edition)

Unwin, S., *The Truth About A Publisher* (George Allen & Unwin, 1960)

White, M., *Tolkien, A Biography* (Little, Brown And Company, 2001)